AF540430

MEDIA EDUCATION

MEDIA EDUCATION

Dr. Shanmukha Rao Padala
Dr. N.V.S. Suryanarayana
Mrs. Goteti Himabindu

A P H PUBLISHING CORPORATION
4435-36/7, ANSARI ROAD, DARYA GANJ
NEW DELHI-110 002

Published by
S.B. Nangia
A P H Publishing Corporation
4435-36/7, Ansari Road, Darya Ganj
New Delhi-110002
Ph. 23274050
Email : aphbooks@gmail.com

2025

Printed at :
Balaji Offset
Navin Shahdara,
Delhi-32

Contents

ABOUT THE BOOK

Media is the means to achieve Excellency in all walks of life. Everyone should realize its importance in this millennium and make the best utilization of all components of media technology for the development of humankind and better living. This book contains nine interesting chapters covering all the areas of media and education. It is very useful for Students, Teachers, Parents, Administrators, Researchers, Policymakers, as well as Youth and for the performance enhancement of the Media.

ABOUT THE AUTHORS

Dr. SHANMUKHA PADALA : The author is a well qualified with M.Com (Accountancy), M.B.A (Human Resources Management), M.Phil and Ph.D in Management. He posses Vast teaching experience in Degree and PG level Teaching. He has great interest in the field of Human Resource Management and Accountancy. Now he is working as Faculty in the Department of Commerce and Management Studies, Andhra University Campus, Vizianagaram. He participated in National and International Seminars, Workshops, Symposias, FDP Programmes and published rich number of articles in reputed journals.

Dr. N.V.S.SURYANARAYANA : The author is an eminent person in the field of Education. Presently he is working as Faculty in the Department of Education, Andhra University Campus, Vizianagaram. He has rich experience in the field of Teacher Education about a decade at Post Degree and PG level. He is having so many degrees and Diplomas like M.Sc (Applied Psychology), M.Sc (Chemistry), M.Sc (Geology), M.Sc (IT), M.A. (Philosophy), M.A (English Literature), M.A (Telugu Literature), M.A (Child Care and Education), M.Ed, M.Phil (Education), and Ph.D in the Field of Educational Psychology. He also Posses PGDCA, PGDEPM, PGDIPM, CFA, CPFN, Certificate in Guidance and Counseling through IGNOU. He is very much fascinated to Psychology and very much interested in Educational Psychology and Guidance & Counseling. He participated in so many National and International Seminars, Workshops, Refresher Courses, Symposia's and published so many articles in reputed Journals. He produced a number of M.Ed and M.Phil Dissertations. He wrote so many books on recent trends in education and innovative Psychological concepts. He is leading the Vizianagaram Unit as **General Secretary** of Andhra Pradesh Progressive Psychologists Association. And Honorary advisor for various Schools and Colleges. For any quarries/suggestions you may contact the author through.

Mrs. GOTETI HIMABINDU : The author is a well qualified Teacher having so many Degrees like M.A (Politics), M.A. (Public Administration), M.A. (Education), M.Li.Sc, M.Ed., M.Phil (Political Science), and now she is doing her Ph.D. She posses good experience in the field of teaching and Research. She has great interest in the field of Education/Psychology/Politics and Contemporary issues and she is doing Educational/Career Counseling. Now she is working as a Faculty in the Department of Political Science, Andhra University Campus, Vizianagaram. She conducted so many Pre service/in-service Training Programmes. She participated in so many National and International Seminars, Workshops, Refresher Courses, Symposia's and published so many articles in reputed Journals.

Introduction

The concept of the media center or learning resource center provides for integrated use of all media. In education, the secondary schools have led the way in this approach to learning. Many of the community colleges are moving towards the concept of integrated media use, but he four-year program is changing more slowly, and in many colleges the audio-visual department is entirely separate from the library.

Media literacy education is at watershed moment around the world. A growing number of countries are developing media education programs in their schools. Media educators from around the world are meeting more often to share curricula, research and strategies. Representatives from nearly 60 countries attended, make this the largest gathering of media educators in history in 2000. Media education is the entitlement of every citizen in every country in the world to freedom of expression and to information and is instrumental in building and sustaining democracy. Media education should be introduced whenever possible within national curricula as well as in tertiary, non-formal and lifelong education. Many positive media literacy developments of today are worth nothing. In addition to new organizations promoting media literacy, a growing number of states have added media literacy goals to their education standards. The considerable presence of media analysis goals in the areas of health and consumer skills also surprised us.

A great deal of publicity is being given to high technology in education, particularly micro-computers and video-discs. There is a danger though that these developments are diverting attention away from the effects of equally powerful low-cost technology. Audio recording is not new education, nor glamorous, but the development of cheap, easy-to-use audio-cassette equipment has already had a major impact on the use of educational broadcasting, both in schools and adult education.

Most of the media program will be implemented outside the center itself, to facilitate and enrich the instruction in the classroom. 'The educational program of the school is strengthened in direct proportion to the quality of the school's library service,' said the 1960 Pennsylvania Governor's Committee on Education. The statement is as valid today as it was then. Today, the media specialist is a teacher in the best sense organizing and maintaining a materials collection. He works directly with teachers and students to achieve educational excellence.

The call fro media education in the United States dates back to the 1950s and the 1970s, when many critical viewing programs were developed, if not back to 1916, when psychologist Hugo Munsterberg called for the serious study, in schools, of the new medium of film, which he called 'The Photoplay'. One of the significant developments in the history of US media education occurred in December 1992 when the Aspen Institute brought 25 educators and activists together for a National Leadership Conference. The group established a definition of media education and a vision for developing it in US education, stating that a media-literate person should be able to access, analyze, evaluate and produce both print and electronic media.

A good background reading before progressing to other books in the bibliography is Robert M.W. Travers' Essentials of Learning: An Overview for Students of Education. An excellent book of background readings which analyse selected factors underlying the process of individualized learning is R.A. Weisgerber's Perspectives in Individualized Learning. An excellent film – which shows the work of Howard kindler or New York University, Tracy Kendler of Barnard College, Kenneth Spence of the State University of Iowa, Harry Harlow of the University of Wisconsin and B.F. Skinner of Harvard is Learning about learning.

Here we discuss about the past research literature concerned with the impact of the media on children and young people. While, there is a particular focus on computer games and the internet. The research on these issues is set in the context of a broad account of research relating to older media, particularly television. In line with the remit of the Byron review the focus here is on negative effects i.e., on the potential harm to children. However, attempts to address negative effects e.g., through various forms of regulation or intervention may also have consequences for positive effects. The report therefore also seeks to address some of the research into the beneficial effects of these media.

Ofcom and other s funders have recently sponsored a comprehensive review of research on harm and offence in media content and an update of that review is currently in progress. Ofcom's review focuses on a broader range of media and is not confined to children and young people. Meanwhile, other more or less definitive reviews specifically relating to games and the internet have also have been produced in recent years. This report does not attempt to duplicate these, but rather to build upon them and to provide a more general commentary on the field of research that will be accessible to the intelligent lay reader. This is not therefore a first hand review of all available studies, although it does incorporate a more original review of emerging developments in the field.

This report seeks to be cautious and even-handed, but it does adopt a rather critical stance towards research, both about the negative effects of these media, and about positive ones. It must certainly prove frustrating to the general reader and indeed to policy-makers seeking to develop an evidence-based approach that research in the field appears so inconclusive and so fraught with disputes and disagreements. Our aim here is partly to explain why that should be the but also to suggest some ways of moving ahead.

The discussing about this attempt is made that the broader social and historical context of research on children and media. It then moves on to outline a possible typology of media effects and to discuss the contribution of two main research traditions in the field. Also review previous research on computer games and the internet, while another issue is new and emerging aspects of these phenomena and their implications for young people. Finally concludes the roles of media literacy both in schools and in the home.

The film is available from State University Film Service, 1400 Washington Avenue, Albany, New York. It shows the different strategies employed by these men in developing new theoretical concepts about man's ability to learn and demonstrates the effect of their theories work upon methods of instruction in schools and colleges. Instruction and learning encompass many processes, many that are not included in learning theories specifically. Instruction involves such considerations as stimulating recall, guiding the learning, gaining and controlling attention, aiding remembering, providing feedback and assessing outcomes. Ultimately, it is the learner who performs such functions. Carefully designed combinations of media best serve the teacher and the school to achieve the kind of learning that is most effective. Robert Glaser, in a number of reports issued through the Learning Research and Development Center, University of Pittsburgh, stressed the concept of learning as education for individuals. The University of Pittsburgh Learning Research and Development Center is an important source for up-to-date information on individualized instruction and learning. In this bibliography, basic background readings on learning are included to provide students of education with an overview of current knowledge.

The Aspen Group also proposed the following precepts:

- Media are constructed and construct reality.
- Media have commercial implications.
- Media have ideological and political implications.
- From and content are related in each medium, each of which has a unique aesthetic, codes and conventions.
- Receivers negotiate meaning in media.

Media literacy involves critically analyzing media messages, evaluating sources of information for bias and credibility, raising awareness of how media messages influence people's belief, attitudes and behaviours and producing messages using different forms of media. Children throughout the world spend an average of three hours each day watching television. At this rate, by the time they reach age 75 they will have spent nine years watching Television. In the US they will have spent two of those nine years watching television ads. When we add the number of hours young people spend watching movies, listening to music and radio and surfing the Internet, they easily devote one-third to one-half of our waking lives to electronic media. Yet many schools still treat poetry, short stories and the novel as the only forms of English expression worthy of study. As a result, most children are not media literate, so they are poorly equipped to engage actively and think critically about the very media that most affect their lives.

Although schools systems throughout the United States are mandated to teach critically thinking, if the schools are not linking this skill to the media world in which so many students are spending upwards of six hours a day, they leaving a potential gold mine unexplored. Most anyone who has engaged in media literacy instruction knows that, before long, parents will report that their children are no longer watching television in the same way they did before. Indeed, parents often remark that after instruction in media literacy, their children constantly point out things while they watch movies or TV programs. They identify jump suts, fades and voiceovers. They detect bias and the power of words to shift meaning and of music to alter the viewer's mood.

Television viewing – which formerly involved relatively passive reception– now involves much more mental activity. Willingly, although without knowing it, the student is now spending a good chunk of those three hours of daily television viewing engaged in critical thinking. The same thing can happen when they are surfing the Net, listening to radio, watching movies, reading the newspaper or playing video games. This is not to say that they will be engaged in critical analysis every moment, but they will be using their higher critical faculties much more if they have been given some of the basic to old of media literacy, of media analysis, than if they have not. We know of no evidence that more critical appraisal undermines one's enjoyment of television or film. To the contrary, understanding how television shows and film are made enhances enjoyment. In some cases, one's tastes may eventually run to less obvious or more sophisticated material, but there is no reasons to expect that a media literate person can't still enjoy the media and derive pleasure and information simultaneously. If schools want students to spend more time thinking critically and practicing critical thinking skills, then they are missing the boat if they are not teaching media literacy and using the media as a site for this critical analysis.

Edgar Dale has said that 'every classroom can have the best in instructional materials now produced' but even if the schools instructional materials are less than excellent, they must be well-organised and administered for effective use.

The library is the center of the program and must lead the way to effective use of educational media. A fine, attractive learning resources center is not the only answer. Teacher must be led to, informed about, and must make use of book and non-book resources to be found in the center. The program of the media center must be planned also to meet the varying and different needs of students. It is the responsibility of the school librarian or media specialist to formulate the objectives of the specific media program, the sum total of all services and learning involved in the center. This must be based upon full and effective participation in the school's curriculum planning. One objective must be to stimulate and guide students and teachers in the uses of media. Another of the opportunity for creative uses of media, to recommend and suggest to students appropriate uses of all media as they work in the center or library. It is necessary that teachers be involved in the selection of media as well as in utilisation. To effectively use media as in integral part of the classroom instruction, teachers must know what is available, have previewed the materials, and have access to the needed equipment and materials.

The Presidential Commission on Instructional Technology offers the following: 'Educational technology is a systematic way of designing, carrying out and evaluating the total process of learning and teaching in terms of specific objectives, based on research in human learning and communication and employing a combination of human and non-human resources to bring about more effective instruction'. Whichever definition is chosen, the important aspect is that education is a systematic process within the framework of educational technology or educational media, a process with a purpose. The purpose of curriculum design is to bring about more effective learning, to solve educational problems, to design effective instruction.

There is a variety of definition of educational technology or educational media. The Random House Dictionary defines Technology as 'the application of knowledge to practical ends, as in a practical ends, as in a particular field: established a National Center for Educational Technology. In our schools and libraries we are most concerned with media, many resources which are used in teaching and learning. Hence, the name educational media, the Department of Audiovisual Instruction Commission on definition and terminology has this definition: 'Educational technology is that field of educational theory and practice primarily concerned with the design and use of messages which control the learning process.' The term audiovisual communication was the label formerly used.

Curriculum development must be systematic if students are to learn to the maximum. We are a goal-oriented society. Whereas most curriculum planning has traditionally been concerned with concept, design for learning in the classroom and school to day is based upon objectives. Educational technology is concerned with curriculum design emphasizing objectives, as well as with methods, materials and evaluation. A Maugham Lee, writing in Audiovisual Instruction, states that 'instructional development seems to hold the greatest promise yet for a way to improve instruction and promote more efficient learning in our increasingly complex and technological society and without compounding the very problem that we are trying to solve'. The purpose of design as a function is to translate general education technology theory and research, as well as subject-matter content, into specifications for learning resources.

Design is not as broad a term as development; development includes production and evaluation functions as well as design.

Students enjoy mediated instruction, they do learn and their varying needs can be met through the use of many media. But media must be a part of planned instruction, and we must have clearly stated objectives. This bibliography emphasizes the importance of design in the curriculum, and the place media has in learning in our schools. We will 'manage' learning as we consider planning controlling, organizing and uses of media. It is the teacher and his new concept of teaching and learning that will change education. It is not the machine but how and why media are used that is important.

Librarians and teachers work together when selecting resources to support the program of the school. A librarian must be knowledgeable of the educational program of a school this is a time-consuming task but important as one aims to provide educational media for the total school program. He must consult with the administration as well as with individual teachers; he must analyse course content and know textbooks well, and must analyse course content and activities to be included in each unit plan. He must know his students, their needs, interests, goals, abilities and concerns. He must match materials with needs; offer services designed to make those materials effective teaching resources in the school. Evaluation involves definition decision-making, values and criteria, administrative levels and the research model.

The items listed in this chapter deal basically with education and learning as related to educational technology. There are references which discuss the major theories of learning in the twenty-first century. Emphasis is upon books which attempt to answer the question of what is known about the process of learning which can be used to design better education in our schools and for individual students.

The winter 1974 issue of School Media Quarterly introduced, in its current Research Column, a listing of 'School Media Dissertations in Progress'. The idea for this came from the Journal of Education for Librarianship, which lists 'Doctoral Dissertations Topics Accepted in Library and Information Science'. The editors of School Media Quarterly hope to develop a listing of school media, dissertations which will tap non-library/information science programs and isolate the school media dissertations found in the JEL list. This current-awareness listing of dissertations on the school library media program is a step toward creating more interest in media research. Much more research in educational media and technology is needed to define and implement solutions to the needs in education today. In research, media is defined broadly as including all print and non-print aids to instruction. Research is needed, in both education and librarianship, on educational media and technology, its uses, preparation, selection, distribution, research, preserves and in-service education, design and evaluation. Good's Dictionary of Education 'study and investigation in the field of education or bearing upon educational problems'.

A more specific one is 'an inquiry-oriented activity employing an objective, empirical and controlled methodology, the findings of which must be replicable when subjected to scrutiny by other investigators, must instill a high level of confidence and must be generalized beyond the local setting in which they are obtained'. The systems approach is a methodology which shows promise in research in new classes of education endeavors. Systems technology has strengthened educational research, and research can make a contribution in educational systems, engineering: the two, in a sense are complementary. The systems approach as research methodology denotes a collection of procedures directed toward realistic effects. Systems, methodology may enable the researcher to focus on larger phenomena and hence produce findings of broad significance. The value of a research study or a systems design, however, depends always upon the researcher's ability ro abstract effectively from the 'rich complexity of reality'.

Application of Media Education

Promoting Democracy

Research has shown that media literacy activities in social studies classes significantly promote civic participation and increase regular newspaper readership among teenagers. With the incredible rise of the internet and the unedited nature of many websites, students need more than ever to learn how to assess the validity and credibility of the information to which they exposed. Our political life became increasingly mediated in the middle of the last century, and now certainly in campaigns and elections, and in day-to-day governance– the media could hardly be more crucial to how we view politicians and our leaders, and how we think about the critical issues of the day. Should we go to war? How will we protect the environment? Will we be taxed more or less? These and every other vital question in our democracy are raised and debated, often superficially, in the nation's media.

Politicians have become extraordinarily adept at using the media to their advantage. If their interests are in line with the nations, this can result in effective government. But as often as not, well-intended or not, vast distortions take place in our public life that are partly a function of how our media systems operate. To the degree that the media are used to propagandize or manipulate and therefore interfere with the public being well informed, we need media education to be part of our schools' civics and social studies classes. No student should leave high school without knowing the classic techniques of persuasion and propaganda, many of which have been taught for decades, but not to all students. Students should be able to recognize 'name-calling', 'bandwagon' and 'glittering generalities' in the arguments they hear and read. But this is only the most basic of beginnings.

Promoting health

Media literacy techniques are also being used increasingly in programs designed to promote health and prevent substance abuse among young people. Indeed, the education represents 'a simple, effective approach to combating the myriad of harmful media messages seen or heard by children and adolescents'. Media literacy approach can also be used in programs focused on conflict resolution and the reduction of aggression and violence. Middle or high school students can be asked, for example, to view part of a film depicting a growing conflict between two rival gangs in a school. The film is stopped, and the students are then assigned to groups to write the next scene, wherein the characters resolve the conflict through talk, rather than with fists, knives or guns. The assignment prompts students to think through how a conflict might be peaceably resolved. Then, in sharing their solutions, the class has the opportunity to hear a variety of solutions. This increases the like hood that some of these solutions will be mentally available should students become involved in a similar conflict.

With the rise of the internet, access is more important than ever, not only should students be able to access the World Wide Web, they should also receive instruction in how to assess the value and validity of websites in all areas, whether medical, political or educational. Now that most anyone can create their own website, a great deal of freedom has been accorded citizens who comes a new and increasing demand on our educational systems and on caregivers to help young people use the internet and all other media-critically and thoughtfully.

One way to integrate media literacy with traditional literacy is to emphasize writing skills in students' scripts and in their critical reviews of films, TV programs, advertising and websites. One way to increase students' interest in literature is to help them recognize that many of the same storytelling techniques used in the classics is also used in the popular programs and films with which they are already familiar. Students already respond to foreshadowing in a television series like Malcolm in the Middle or a movie like Spiderman; they are often simply unaware that foreshadowing is a deliberate technique used to heighten suspense, drama and irony. Knowing the terms and being able to apply them is more important than some might think. Knowing about foreshadowing, symbolism, character development and other techniques used in literature and in film and television permits greater appreciation of the art forms.

Prevention of public health problems

Today most prevention practitioners and researchers, as well as concerned teachers and parents recognise that many of the messages we get from the media are risk factors for numerous public health problems. From the time we wake up to the radio alarm clock to the time we fall asleep with the TV on, we live in a media culture. We cannot escape the media's influence on either our healthy or unhealthy behaviours. Numerous studies over the past five decades have examined the impact of media on children, with regard to such risky behaviours as violence, alcohol, tobacco and other drug abuse, poor body image and eating disorders, precocious, unsafe sexual activity and teen pregnancy. More than 1,000 studies have looked at the effects of violence in television and movies, including the three-year National Television Violence Study completed in 1998. Most of these studies conclude that children who watch significant amounts of television and movie violence are more likely than children who see media violence to exhibit aggressive behaviour, attitudes and values.

The pervasiveness of the media, there are neurological reasons that we do not perceive the influence of the media. Brain research demonstrates that we respond to images differently than we respond to print. When we read books, we process the text in the neocortex and the process is slow and thoughtful. When we process images, we do it in the limbic system and the process is very rapid through instinct, impulse and emotion. This is the same part of the brain that produces the fight or flight response, which gets our adrenalin pumping without our conscious thought. Critical thinking is necessary to media literacy as a prevention strategy. The goal of media literacy in prevention is to move our responses to media images out of the limbic system and into the neocortex, where we can respond more thoughtfully and carefully to the messages the images are giving us. Media literacy allows youth to reflect on important life choices and make decisions about their health behaviours. It allows young people to control the influences of media messages instead of controlled by them.

Emerging development of Mass Media

The mass media reader edited by Wardrip-Fruin and Montfort defines new/mass media by using eighth simple and concise propositions.

1. *New media versus cyber culture:* cyber culture is the study of various social phenomena that are associated with the internet and network communications, whereas new/mass media is concerned more with cultural objects and paradigms.

2. *New media as computer technology used as a distribution platform:* new/mass media are the cultural objects which use digital computer technology for distribution and exhibition. E.g., internet, web sites, computer multimedia, blue-ray disks etc. The problem with this is that the definition must be revised every few years. The term 'new/mass media' will not be new anymore as most forms of culture will be distributed through computers.
3. *New media as digital data controlled by software:* The language of new media is based on the assumption that, infact, all cultural objects that rely on digital representation and computer-based delivery do share a number of common qualities. New media is reduced to digital data that can be manipulated by software as any other data. Now media operations can create several versions.
4. *New meida as the mix between existing cultural conventions and the conventions of software:* new media today can be understood as the mix between older cultural conventions for data representation, access and manipulation and newer conventions of data representation, access and manipulation, e.g., in film, software is used in some areas of production, in others are created using computer animation.
5. *New media as the Aesthetics that accompanies the early stage of every new modern media and communication technology:* while ideological tropes indeed seem to be reappearing rather regularly, many aesthetic strategies may reappear two or three times. In order for this approach to be truly useful it would be insufficient to simple name the strategies and tropes and to record the moments of their appearance instead, we would have to develop a much more comprehensive analysis which would cooelate the history of technology with social, political, environmental and economical histories or the modern period.
6. *New media as faster execution of algorithms previously executed manually or through other technologies:* Computers are a huge speed-up of what weere previously manual techniques. E.g., calculators. Dramatically speeding up the

execution makes possible previously non-existent representational technique. This also make possible of many ne forms of medi art such as interactive multimedia and computer games. On one level, a modern digital computer is just a faster calculator, we should not ignore it's other identity, that of a cybernetic control device.

7. *New média as the encoding of modernist avant-garde, new media as metamedia*: Manovich declares that the 1920s are more relevant to new media than any other time period, Meta media coincides with postmodernism in that they both rework old work rather than create new work. New media avant-garde is about new ways of accessing and manipulating information. Meta-media is an example of how quantity can change into quality as in new technology and manipulation techniques can recode modernist aesthetics into a very different postmodern aesthetics.

8. *New media as parallel articulation of simlar ideas in post-world war II art and modern computing*: post world war II art or combinationtorics involves creating images by systematically changing a single parameter. This leads to the creation or remarkably similar images and spatial structures. This illustrates that algorithms, this essential part of new media do not depend on technology, but can be executed by humans. Moreover, the emerging trends of mass media is numerous, heterogeneous and multifaceted. We the communication specialists have named the all the emerging mass media trends as new media. It is a term meant to encompass the emergence of digital, computerized or networked information and communication technologies in the later part of the 20th century. Most technologies described as new media are digital, often having characteristics of being manipulated, networkable, dense compressible, interactive and impartial. Some examples may be the internet, websites, computer multimedia, computer games, CD-Roms and DVDs.

Negative effects of Media

Looking across the research literature, one can see that a very wide range of potentially negative effects of media have been identified and discussed. These would include effects relating to:

- Violence contenty including imitation in the form of aggression or anti-social behaviour, desebsitisation and fear.
- Sexual content includes imitation in the form of promiscuous or unsafe practices, arousal and shock or disgust.
- Advertising in relation to misleading claims as well as consumerist or materialistic atttudes more broadly.
- Inappropriate or unwanted contract with others for example in the form of stranger danger or bullying.
- Health e.g., to do with smoking, alcohol and drug-taking .
- Eating behaviour– in relation to both obesity and eating disorders
- General personality disorders, such as low self-esteem, identity confusion or alienation.
- Physical effects of excessive use e.g, RSI type conditions and eyesight problems relating to computers.
- The undermining of children's imagination and free play.
- The physical development of the brain and disorders such as attention deficit and hyperactivity.
- Sleeping problems and other behavioural difficulties reduced for family interaction or relationships with peers
- Reduced levels of educational achievement or reading more specifically.
- Mistaken values, attitudes or beliefs e.g., in relation to gender or ethnic stereotyping.

While there is clearly a danger here of generating an endless litany of the evils wronght by the media. It is important to recognise that different types of potential effects are frequently confused or conflated often in quite contradictory ways. This is perhaps clearest in the case of debates about media violence. Researchers in this field have explored a very wide range of potential effects of media violence and generated some very different theories to explain how these ocuur. A short list of such theories are:

- Imitation: people identify with attractive role models they encounter in the media and learn specific patterns of aggressive behaviour from them.
- Arousal: people are emotional and/or physically aroused by media in general and this increased level of excitement can lead to aggressive behaviour.
- Desensitisation: repearted exposure to media violence dulls people's responses to the effects of violence in real life and thus leads them to regard it as acceptable.
- Catharsis: viewing violence can reduce or even purge aggressive tendencies or psychological tensions that people already possess.
- Cultivation: the media portray violence in systematically distorted ways e.g., in terms of its frequency or who perpetrated it, which leads people to have distored beliefs about the real wold.

Again, this list is not exhaustive. Even so, just in this one area we find a range of competing and potentially contradictory hypotheses. Different theories propose different mechanisams through which such effects might be assumed to occur and behind this there are potentially quite different ideas of what would count as violent or aggressive in the first place. In broad terms, it would be helpful to distinguish here between three potential types of negative effects. We could illustrate these with examples relating to the effects of sexual content:

- Behavioural exposure to sexual content might lead people to copy what they see, to seek out situations in which they might be able to copy it, or alternatively to avoid it.
- Attitudinal: such exposure might lead people to develop particular beliefs e.g., about the situations in which sexual activity is appropriate or morally acceptable or about the desirable behaviour of men and women.
- Emotional: people might obviously become aroused by sexual content, but they might equally be shocked disgusted or even traumatised.

These three types of effects are clearly not mutually exclusive. They might well reinforce each other, although equally they might contradict each other. For example emotional effects might have behavioural consequences. Disgust at sexual images might lead one to avoid potential sexual encounters, just as feelings of fear aroused by media violence might lead people to avoid conflict in real life. In addition, it is important to make other types of distinctions among potential media effects. These would include:

- Short-term and long-term: some types of effects might build up over a long period, last a long time and be hard to displace while others might be more immediately intense, but might fade more quickly.
- Individual or social: some types of effects might apply primarily to individuals, while others might apply more to particular social groups than others or function on a more general societal level.
- Direct or indirect: some effects might be direct and of a stimulus-response variety, while others might work through other factors rather than immediately on the individual.

These different hypotheses and approaches also translate into different research methodologies e.g., in the case of violence, laboratory experiments are typically concerned with measuring relatively short-term effects on behaviour. They do not in themselves provide sufficient evidence about long-term effects e.g., that watching violence at one point will result in violent behaviour at some later point. Researchers concerned with the impact of violence on attitudes or beliefs are more inclined to use surveys in which people report their own media use although these often have difficulty identifying the specific contribution of the media to the formation of such beliefs. Researchers looking at shorter-term emotional responses may sometimes employ physiological measures these typically provide very little evidence about the meanings people attribute to the media or the reasons why they respond in the way they do.

Media is quite useful in fostering development. In the past it has been seen that media has not played its role in accelerating development. Only recently some sections of the media have tried to bring out deficiencies in achieving millennium development goals. Media has not able to drive into the minds of the ordinary people – what is millennium development goal? People at large, particular the poor do not understand human development index. It is necessary to make people aware about their role in improving their own quality of life and Human Development Index. All development programmes of the central and the state government are not known to the people for whom these programs are meant. They do not know the purpose of different schemes launched to improve the quality of lives of poor people in particular. Such ignorance leads to information blackout for the poor. Government functionaries at the grass root level deliberately conceive such information from the target group beneficiaries. The poor man is required to pay information brokers to get information about the schemes. There after the poor has to pay the power brokers moving around the power centres in rural areas to get their legitimate rights like old age pension, India Awas Yojana, NRHM, SC & ST scholarship, opportunities to work public distribution system etc.

Now-a-days media is increasingly becoming commercial in nature leaving little space for vital information meant for the poor. Being the fourth pillar in functioning of democracy media should be responsible to disseminate vital information to the poor by devoting adequate space for the purpose. With the advent of technology and mobile connectivity it is also necessary to collect information from the poor regarding their miserable plight. Media houses should create voice mail based blogs to enable the poor to air their views regarding the benefits reaching them or otherwise. It is possible to create facilities to get public feedback through mobiles which can be collated to generate interest in news items for the benefit of government functionaries and public.

The youth people of our country are enthusiastic and can be encouraged to act as citizen reporters on developmental issues concerning the lives of the poor. The role of the youth in generating awareness about anti-poverty programmes and employment opportunities is of paramount importance. Young people should come forward to collect and pass on to the media in relevant news on improvement of deficiencies in implementation of welfare programmes concerning human development indexes.

2

Media Education in Indian Society

In last 50 years the media influence has grown exponentially with the advance of technology, first there was the telegraph, then the radio, the newspaper, magazines, television and now the internet. We live in a society that depends on information and communication to keep moving in the right direction and do out daily activities like work, entrainment, health care, education, personal relationships, traveling and anything else that we have to do. A common person in the society usually wakes up checks the television news or newspaper, goes to work, makes a few phone calls, eats with their family when possible and makes his decisions based on the information that he has either from their co-workers, news, TV, friends, family, financial reports etc.

What we need to be aware is that most of our decisions, beliefs and values are based on what we know for a fact, our assumptions and our experience. In our work we usually know what we have to do base on our experience and studies, however, on our daily lives we rely on the media to get the current news and facts about what is important and what we should be aware of. We have put our trust on the media as an authority to give us news, entertainment and education.

The media makes billions of dollars with the advertising they sell and that we are exposed to. We buy that we are told to be good, after seeing thousands of advertisings we make our buying decisions based on what we saw on TV, newspapers or magazines to be a product we can trust and also based on what everyone else that we know is buying and their decision are also base on the media. These are the effects of mass media in teenagers, they buy what they see on TV, what their favorite celebrity advertise and what is acceptable by society based on the fashion that the media has imposed them.

Here is a positive influence example, if there is a sport that getting a lot of attention by the media and gains popularity among your friends and society, you will more likely want to practice the sport and be cool with all your friends. The result is that you will have fun with your friends and be more healthy because of the exercise your doing. Recent example is world cup hockey being watched by millions due to the advertisement and publicity in media which also increased TRP and desire of many people to watch our national sport.

However a negative influence in teenagers is the use of cigars by celebrity movie stars, the constant exposure of sex images, the excessive images of violence and exposure to thousands of junk food ads. Young people are in a stage of life where they want to be accepted by their peers, they want to be loved and be successful. The media creates the ideal image of a beautiful men and women and tells you what the characteristics of a successful person are; you can see it in movies and TV. It's a subliminal way to tell you that are not like them you are not cool yet so its time to buy the stuff they buy and look like they look.

Another negative influence in teenagers that has grown over the years are anorexia and obesity. There are millions of adolescents fighting obesity, but all the same time they are exposed to thousands of advertisements of junk food, while the ideas image of a successful person is told to be thin and wealthy. Also more women are obsessive with losing weight even they are not obese, these are many thin women that want to look like the super models and thin celebrities so they engage in eating disorders which leads to severe health issues and even death.

Radio and television has been the most economical, long-standing and the most widely used among various electronic media. Despite the arrival of various media options, radio continues to remain as one of the dominant media among the public. Radio and television as a medium for information and communication to the masses is predicted to retain its relevance and potency. In particular its reach and efficacy as an educational medium is finding increasing relevance to students in recent times. It is the most extensive network. Radio and television signals cover almost the entire country. A parallel development sweeping the field of electronic audio media is a successful introduction, meteoric rise and spread of FM radio channels run by both public and private initiatives. Community radio is now booming through out India. Reports confirm that it has supported educational programs in a wide range of subject areas in many different countries.

Review of Media Literacy

The Byron review is assessing a range of potential measures that might be taken to ensure children's safe and productive use of the internet and computer games. These are included regulatory strategies and interventions of various kinds. These possibilities will be carefully evaluated in the light of growing international experience in the field. This final section of the report considers one such strategy, namely the promotion of media literacy. This issue has been addressed extensively in our earlier review for Ofcom, so this section will provide a brief overview of the rationale for this approach and some of the questions that it raises.

Both in the UK and Internationally, media literacy has become an increasingly significant dimension of cultural policy. According to the former Culture Secretary Tessa Jowell, media literacy is an essential component of contemporary citizenship that will eventually become as important skill as Math's or science. Ofcom has a statutory responsibility under the 2003 Communications Acts to promote media literacy, though supporting research, educational and networking activities. The BBC, the film Council, Skill set and the British Film Institute are leading a media Literacy task Force that has produced a media Literacy chapter, which currently has more than 120 institutional signatories. Meanwhile, the European Commission has established a media literacy expert group and will shortly be issuing an official communication on the theme and UNESCO has launched a new policy statement on media literacy following a high-profile meeting in Paris in 2007.

The growing interest in media literacy reflects a new emphasis in regulatory policy. While it is by no means incompatible with content regulation or with government intervention more broadly, the focus here is on empowering consumers to make informed choices and judgments about media on their own behalf. This is a broadly educational strategy, which includes work in schools as well as in the home and in other informal settings. Media literacy is generally conceived as a partnership between government, the media industries, teachers, parents and children themselves.

Ofcom defines media literacy as the ability to access, understand and create communications in a variety of contexts. Media literacy is partly able to locate and use media, but it is also about critical understanding evaluation and judgment and about creating media for the purpose of communication and self-express. Promoting literacy is therefore about addressing basic inequalities in people's access to media not only the so called digital divide, but also divides in relation to other media as well. Ultimately these divides are not simply about access to equipment, they are also about cultural capital about the skills and understanding that people need in order to use and interpret what they see and hear and to create their own communications.

Beyond extending access, a basic first step in media literacy is informing consumers, in case of the concerns of this review, this point to the crucial role of content labeling. Much of the democratic potential of the modern media derives from the fact that gatekeepers or intermediaries are no long have such powerful control, yet it is also from this that much of the risk and potential for harm derives. In this new environment, there is an increasingly important role for labeling and classification systems that inform parents and children about what they are likely to encounter. This should be seen not only in negative terms as a matter of warnings or guidance but also more positively, as a matter of alerting people to content that they might find particularly valuable. The contemporary proliferation of media has generated new risks, but it has also led to the production of a great deal of positive material that could never have been created or distributed before some of it made by children themselves. One of the key challenges that parents and children face is simply finding out what is available and knowing where to locate it.

There is a long tradition of media education in UK schools, although it has remained fairly marginal to the mainstream curriculum, particularly in primary schools. Paradoxically, media literacy has not been a significant element of the National Literacy Strategy and the National curriculum for information and communication technology currently focuses primarily on technical skills rather than on the evaluation of digital content. By contrast, media educators have a well-established conceptual framework and a developed set of classroom strategies, that increasingly need extended to digital media such as computer games and the internet. Media education involves understanding the processes by which media are produced, analyzing the verbal and visual languages' they use to create meaningful judgment about how media represent the world and understanding how audiences are targeted and how they respond. These approaches generally involve both critical study and creative production of media. As digital media have become more and more accessible and easy to use, teachers have found that children can develop critical understanding in a more engaging, hands-on way by making media themselves. While there is a considerable body of professional know-how among specialist teachers in this field, there remains a need for in-depth evaluation of the effectiveness of media education and for a more systematic approach across the age range.

I relation to new media, there have been several educational initiatives addressing aspects of online risk. There is now a plethora of websites and educational resources in the field produced by a wide range of voluntary sector and industry bodies as well as by government agencies. Evidence of the effectiveness of these initiatives is rather limited and somewhat mixed; much depends on the training of teachers and on the involvement of parents. Some research suggests that a greater awareness of risk does not necessarily lead children to adopt less risky behaviour and this in turn points to the need for approaches that connect more effectively with children's everyday experiences of these media. In the light of contemporary developments of the kind strategies also need to adopt broader approach; children need to be aware of stranger danger, but they also need to understand the commercial strategies that are being used online and develop skills in critically evaluating online content. Here again, the experience on such issues could usefully be drawn together and evaluated at this stage and more coherent strategic devised.

The new media pose much wider challenges for educators. In addition to addressing inequalities in access to technology and in the competencies that are required to use it, educators also need to be exploring some of the new ethical issues posed by new media and the ways in which online content needs to be assessed and evaluated. In this respect, they will need to look beyond narrow conceptualizations of digital literacy that see it simply in terms of safety or technical skill and to address much broader questions about how these media are produced, circulated and consumed. Such approach would need to address issues of trust and credibility, but it would also need to analyze the social, political and economic dimensions of technology. Further it should be emphasized that media literacy is not simply concerned with information, but also with media as art forms with intrinsic and lasting value. Many computer games and online worlds offer rich and complex symbolic environments; and the experience of play is often very emotionally intense. Likewise, some forms of online communication and the creation of user generated content can involve profound issues of identity, self-representation and personal investment. Media literacy also involves reflecting on these cultural experiences and the pleasures that they entail, here again, addressing the risks that may be at stake in young people's use of media must involve an understanding of the reasons why they often deliberately choose to take them.

Parents can clearly play a key role in developing media literacy. However, we should be way of assuming that parents necessarily possess such skills and knowledge themselves, particularly when it comes to new media, media literacy is an issue for adults too, as Ofcom's report on this issue makes clear. Regulatory devices such as filters or age verification systems or legislative constraints such as those introduced in the US under the children's online protection and privacy act are unlikely to be effective if parents are unable to operate the technology are unaware of what their children might be doing online. Research suggests that parental monitoring and involvement can make a difference to children's awareness of issues such as safety, but this need to be handled sensitively, in a way that respects young people's right to privacy and does not place an undue burden on parents themselves.

Simply sharing and discussing experiences of game-playing and online participation can be a valuable starting point. Here too, there is a need to develop constructive approaches that are positively child centered and in tune with the realities of everyday family life, and the basis for this should be dialogue with parents and children themselves. Finally, it is important to emphasize that media literacy is not an alternative to regulation as is sometimes implied. People who are more media literate are not necessarily immune to harm or to media influence more broadly. The primary aim of media literacy education is not to reduce the influence of the media, any more than the aim of literacy education is to reduce the influence of books. Rather, it seeks to enable children to make informed decisions on their own behalf and thereby to make the most of the opportunities that the media can provide.

In 1956, India was site of the famous Pune Radio Farm Forum Project. The United Nations Educational Science and Cultural organization (UNESCO) sponsored 'Pune' Project it was inspired by Canada's experience with radio farm forum in the 1940s. the Pune project was a field experiment to evaluate the effects of radio farm forums, each consisting of several dozens of villagers who gathered weekly to listen to a half-hour radio program and then to discuss its contents.

The All India Radio development programming range is use of entertainment-instruction serials. As defined previously, entertainment instruction was the process of purposely designing and implementing a media message to both entertain and educate, in order to increase audience's knowledge about an educational issue, create favourable attitudes and change overt behaviour. Entertainment-education seeks to capitalize on the popular appeal of entertainment media, in order to show individuals how they can live safer, healthier and happier lives. Since 1987, the Central Educational Broadcasting Unit (CEBU) of All India Radio has produced several entertainments – education.

The National Broadcasting Company transmitted the experimental program from the third floor of the Radio Corporation of America building to 25 receivers watched by the students in 1938. The show was 45 minutes long and students asked questions via a two-way radio communication and were answered by the instructor on the screen. With the expanding and enormous capacity of radio to deliver their goods to the people many new channels have emerged. Moreover, they are working for round the clock in a day. This has encouraged the authorities to start Gyan Darshan on television and GV for radio. These channels are dedicated to transmit educational programs. As per planning of GV in future to start more than hundred FM educational radio stations would come up in the country. In the later planning more FM stations are expected to be allowed for the purpose of education and development.

A study tried to gauze the situation pertaining to radio listening and number of FM sets. It also includes the concept of educational programs on radio. The study having sample of 100 FM radio household in urban area and equal number in rural was recently conducted by All India Radio, Ahmadabad. This suggests that in urban areas there was higher listening compared to rural area. The average listening among total respondents was 85 per cent. Another study was conducted by Kumar, A. (2002) it was found that 15 per cent of academic counselors in the Indira Gandhi National Open University have been using radio programs including GV for their core academic activities. Computers and Internet have started influencing the way we learn. Radio is still a dominant medium with wide access, all these media are very powerful to reach teach and enrich. Basic tips to learn from broadcast and non-broadcast media have been provided.

Reports are confirmed that it has supported educational programs in a wide range of subjects in many different countries. In Thailand, the radio is used to teach mathematics to school children and for teacher training and other curricula. Swaziland, for public health purpose, Columbia for various programs, Nicaragua, for health education and Philippines uses the radio for nutrition education, Sri Lanka, for family planning and health, South Korea, in support of family planning, Botswana for civics education, the Dominion Republic in support of primary education and Paraguay to offer Primary school instruction. The above review suggested that there are number of educational courses that rely on educational radio, more so in case of distance education. Education was become technology and media enable worldwide.

Public Opinion influenced by Media

As we have said above, the media has a huge impact on society and also in public opinion. They can shape the public opinion in different ways depending of what is the objective. For example, after the attacks of 9/11 the media gave a huge coverage of the event and exposed Osama guilty for the attack as they were told by the authorities. This shaped the public opinion to support the war on terrorism, the same happened with the war of Iraq. The problem is that if media received inaccurate information then the public opinion supported a wrong cause, this is the power of public opinion influence.

Other ways to influence are with polls and trends, especially in political campaigns. The candidates that can pay more TV and media exposure have more influence on public opinion and thus can receive more votes. The media shape our attitudes about everything from soap to politics. It's important for us to be aware of the impact the mass media has on each and every one of. We need to be vigilant and ask ourselves to look for opposing opinions and evaluate the facts for ourselves rather than blindly accepting the media's version of the 'truth'.

Everything has been changed due to change in technology and globalization. New media effect and also affect the social behaviour of the people. Basically youth behaviour and their relationship with parents, brothers' sisters and other relatives are being influenced by Mass Media. Today television and internet have become a part of the life of adolescents. Media factionalize people with its mixture of technology. So, electronic media has tremendous impact on youth compared to print media.

Mass media may be defined as any form of communication which effect large number of people at the same time directly in a uniform manner. The mode of communication may be through TV, radio, print media, internet etc it I not consider as a tool of marketing or advertising drive but an instrument to influence the behaviour of mass. Basically it is termed as word-of-mouth channel. So, mass media is considered as a technology tool for masses for providing every type of education to change the life style of the people.

Keeping in mind the above issues, the media should not help to raise crime, vandalism, alcoholism, sex, teenage pregnancy etc. Media plays a very important role in creating awareness. Certain issues which are untouched must be highlighted. The anxieties to know something should be protested in a decent manner. Decency is always praise worthy. It develops peace and brings happiness among various communities which ultimately leads towards the improvement of quality of life of the human beings. Therefore, the role of media should be bring peace and happiness among the audience and try to develop the human values.

Media role to development of India

Media is the means of support to the people in the world which shapes their attitude, opinion and makes them to think before they start doing a particular work. The most beautiful is it helps the people to know about different religions, places, languages important things to do about the past and the future.

Had it not been the media or publicity, Taj Mahal would not have become one of the seven wonder of the world. Had it not been the media we would not be able to see our real heroes, the NSG commandos who saved us from the terrorist attack in Mumbai. Who would have cared or even think of saving our national animal whose count is decreasing day by day to 1411 only for the audience mass media is source of entertainment, for journalists media is source of prestige and salary and for the owner media is source of profit and political influence! It is because the media possesses so much power to influence, that those in the media must be feel their duty about delivering news in a balanced manner that brings the story to the consumer with all sides fairly represented.

All the mediums like the radio, the newspaper, magazines, television and now the internet are bringing the updates of each and every bit of news that is available round the world and now you can also actively take part in the discussion or give your comments by polling, blogging or sending SMS. Certain issues which needs to be discussed or certain questions which needs to be answered by the authority can now are easily done with the help of different media.

Media plays a very important role in creating awareness. There are certain issues which remain untouched among youngsters as they feel guarded concerning it. Media helps in providing information regarding such topics. There are many such topics that are highlighted by the media. The current one that can be talked about is the quota system in colleges. Media created awareness that how injustice was being done with deserving candidates due to reservations in colleges. There was procession taken out by students in order to object regarding this bias discrimination.

One other such issue is the debate carried on regarding sex education. Media was trying to highlight both the aspects of the matter that whether sex education must be allowed in schools or not. There were a group of people who were all for it and there were people who considered it a taboo. Even though we are heading towards westernization, our roots still remain Indian and that is the reason why we fell anxious discussing such issues with young ones. But if we think practically then there are so many instances where children head the wrong way just in the anxiety of knowing certain issues. So, the only acceptable approach in which we can guard our child from choosing the wrong path is by talking to them and educating them about the issues that need to be learnt at the right instance.

Media being one of the important means to reach out masses

and influence their thinking and decision making, only to the positive media cannot attract attention of the masses, and to gain viewer ship, negative media has to be incorporated to balance out and attract the masses, but a line has to be drawn between the positive and the negative media in the interest of the younger generation.

Unfortunately, it is very rare for research to tell a story. Researchers frequently disagree about fundamental issues to do with focus, method and theory about how the key questions are to be framed, what might be able to count as an answer and what the implications of these answers might be in terms of what should be done. Such disagreements are common in many areas, but they are particularly acute in research on media efforts. Historically, there has been a clear distinction between researchers in the psychological effects tradition and those in the fields of media and cultural studies, which are broadly sociological orientation. To some extent, this maps on to a distinction between US researchers and European researchers. However, the situation is a little more complex than this.

It is important to recognize that much of the psychological effects research is based on a particular form of psychology. It generally espouses variants of behaviourism and rarely engages with what is termed cultural psychology. Psychologists in the UK and in the Europe are generally much more circumspect about media effects than psychologists in the US and some are strongly critical of the US approach. There are also several leading cultural studies academics in the US who are equally forthright in their criticisms. There are fundamental differences between these two broad traditions, which are not just a question of different areas of interest or simply to do with methodology. On the contrary, they reflect very basic theoretical and indeed political differences. As a result, the debates in this are have been highly polarized and often somewhat less than constructive. At the risk of merely contributing to this polarization, it is important to sum up some of the differences at this point.

Research Effects

Essentially, researcher in the psychological effects tradition are seeking evidence of more or less direct causal relationship between exposure to media and particular consequences in terms of audiences behaviour or attitudes. A classic behaviourist perspective conceives of this process in terms of stimulus and response of which the most obvious example would be imitation. More sophisticated exponents of this approach posit the existence of intervening variables that come between the stimulus and the response and thereby mediate any potential effects; and there is also some recognition here of individual differences in response. Even the basic cause-and-effect model continues to apply.

This research tends to work with a broadly positivist approach. It generates hypotheses about the social world that are then tested empirically through the application of scientific or mathematical methods and thereby verified or falsified. It is assumed that we can measure aspects of media content quantitatively that we can do the same with audience responses and that we can then correlate these in order to gain some measure of media effects. Potential variables in the process can be isolated and controlled or accounted for statistically and any potential influence of the scientist on the design or interpretation of the study can be eliminated or minimized. These approaches claim to provide predictability, objectivity and a basis for generalization and findings of such research can be statistically aggregated by a technique known as meta-analysis.

With the history of communications research in the United States, the use of such methods has served as a form of what Thomas Kuhn calls 'normal science' i.e., they permit a business as usual approach in which established rules and procedures are followed by all and fundamental theoretically challenges are simply ignored. Thus, most media effects researchers tend to display a considerable degree of certainty about their findings. The effects of media violence e.g., are seen as incontrovertibly proven. There is no room for dispute on the matter. Unfortunately, many other researchers from different research traditions have persistently disputed such claim, although effects researchers have attempted to deal with this largely by refusing to engage in debate.

Criticisms of Effects Research

So what criticisms have been made of such research? Again, at the risk of oversimplification it is possible to sum these up as follows:

1. *The evidence of effects is actually equivocal and contradictory, even on its own terms:* Criticisms effects research point out that journals tend only to publish studies that show positive results. The sizes of effects in such studies are frequently small and the level of statistical significance is often marginal, although far-reaching claims are often made on the basis of what amounts to quite flimsy evidence. Critics argue that studies often contradict each other and hence cannot be meaningfully aggregated e.g., in the case of media violence, proof of desensitization would contradict an argument about arousal and so studies in these two domains cannot be seen to reinforce each other. The most telling criticisms of this kind are often made by fellow psychologists.
2. *There are significant problems with the methods used in effects research:* The two key methods that have been used in this work, laboratory experiments and surveys, have significant and well-known limitations when it comes to proving causal relationships between phenomena in real life. The key problem with laboratory experiments is to do with their artificially or lack of what is termed ecological validity. Critics argue that what happens in the context of a laboratory, where one is seeking to maximize potential effects in order to make them observable, cannot be generalized to the real world. Where a whole range of other factors may be in play. The stimulus material used in such experiments is often unrepresentative of media that would be encountered in real life as are the measures of response. Administrating a fake electric shock to an unknown individual in the context of a laboratory following exposure to a random collection of violent incidents on film and without any of the usual constraints that tend to inhibit aggressive behaviour cannot be seen to prove that media cause violence. At best, laboratory experiments can be seen as an indication of

what might possibly happen, rather than as evidence of what actually does happen in real life.

3. *The notion of 'effect' is itself simplistic and theoretically inadequate:* The term 'effect' clearly implies a cause and effect relationship and beyond that it is frequently associated with an essentially behaviourist account of human action. This is a theoretical approach that some effects research continues to employ, although much of it also seeks to specify 'intervening variables' that mediate between the stimulus and the response. However, critics of effects research seek to challenge the basic theoretical assumptions of this approach.

   The criticisms here are partly about how we understand the nature of the stimulus in other words, what we assume about the meaning of media. Effects research typically presumes that media texts have singular meanings that will be the same for all who encounter them and that those meanings can be straightforwardly quantified. But Barker has argued that false to assume as effects researchers typically do that violence has a fixed meaning irrespective of the ways in which it is represented, who commits it and who is victimized, the motivations for their actions and so on. Research suggests that there are many different types of media violence and that different people perceive different things to be violent in the first place, not least as a result of their different experiences of violence in real life. The broader argument here is that meaning involves interpretation; it cannot be fixed or defined statistically in the ways that positivist approaches tend to assume.

   Critics of effects research also challenge assumptions about the nature of the response. They argue that effects researchers implicitly conceive of media audiences as passive and ignorant victims of media influence. Specific sections of the audience are effectively stigmatized as helpless dupes e.g., in the pathological category of the heavy viewer. This approach to children is particular, where the use of some versions of developmental psychology tends to define children primarily in terms of what they lack i.e., the rationality that is presumed to characterize nature adulthood. Children are thereby defined in terms of what they cannot do, rather than what they can and in the process researchers typically fail to see the issues from children's own perspectives.

4. *Effects research tends to sustain a conservative political agenda:* Behind many of these objections and to some extent motivating them is a broader political argument. Effects research is frequently informed by a conservative moral or political agenda and indeed some of it had been funded by organizations with very clearly defined motivations of this kind. This is most self-evidently the case in research about the effects of sexual content, where researchers moral beliefs are apparent in taken for granted assumptions about promiscuity or healthy sexual behaviour. As I have noted that arguments about media effects have often served to distract attention away from broader social problems and one could argue that as in the case of violence the media are frequently used by politicians as a scapegoat.

The concern here is partly that research helps to sustain a moral consensus in which deviant or marginal tastes and views are suppressed. However, it is also argued that effects research sanctions simplistic and misleading responses to complex social problems rather than looking at a particular social phenomenon such as violence and then seeking to explain it, effects research starts with media and then seeks to trace evidence of their effects on individuals. In this respect, it appears to be asking the questions in the wrong way round.

The debate about media effects can also be of use to politicians who seek to appear tough, blaming the media can help deflect attention away from more deep-seated causes of social problems, which may be more difficult to address at a policy level. The debate about media violence is perhaps the classic instance of this process. This issue has a particularly high profile in the US. There has been a constant succession of governmental inquiries and government-funded research efforts although arguably these have had very little impact on policy. For commentators in other countries, it seems quite obvious that the simplest way of reducing the high incidence of violence in the US would be to restrict the availability of lethal weapons although this is an issue that governments have largely been unwilling or unable to address. In this context, talking tough about media violence provides an easy way of being seen to act.

Role of Media in Indian Democracy

Selection of personal to man the organization is one of the most important managerial responsibilities. The ability of organization to achieve its goal, survive and growth in a dynamic environment significantly and substantially depends upon the effectiveness of its selection process. This is particularly shown in India, as industrial enterprises here are opening in highly dynamic environment conditions. Selection is the next step after recruitment. The selection process involves a series of steps which help in evaluating the candidates. The selection process in an organization has to be in accordance with the organizational requirements. Job analysis and job specifications, along with human resource planning provide the basic requirements, based on which the selection process has to be designed. The process of choosing the most suitable candidate for the job from among the available applicants is called selection.

A manager is a person tasked with overseeing one or more employees or departments to ensure these employees and departments carry out assigned duties as required. Depending on the size of the company there might be a single, dual or triple management layer involved. In large companies management is basically divided into three tires: upper, middle and lower management. Lower management includes managers who operate at basic levels of organization functions. Middle level management overseas lower-management and generates reports for senior management. Upper management commonly consist of a board of directors or shareholders who own and are responsible for making key decisions that affect the organization. In commercial franchises like restaurants, a retail manager ensures the daily business functions smoothly. The office manager might be responsible for a variety of duties commonly divided into individual departments in large organizations. These duties might include accounting, shipping and customer service, where additional employees who act under the office manager carry out most of these tasks.

1. India is federal democratic republic. In a democratic set-up as large as this, the state along with the process of development. Access to information is essential to the health of democracy for at least two reasons: first, it ensures that citizens make responsible and informed choices rather than acting out ignorance or misinformation. Second, information serves 'checking function' by ensuring that elected representatives uphold their oaths of office and carry out wishes of those who elected them.
2. In multi-religious, multi-lingual, multi-cultural and multi-ethnic democratic policy like India, it is not easy for the people like India; it is not easy for the people to identify themselves with the process of change. In this context, the media plays a two way role: on the one hand, of keeping the people informed of the state's policies, development programs and actions on ground and on the other hand, getting the feedback to the planners decision makers and administrators on the reactions and responses of the people. The media is supposed to the mirror in which the state and the people find their reflection.
3. The media in India has also functioned as an instrument of exchange of message between different sections of the people or society between the rural and the urban sectors, industrial and agricultural sector between the majority of the population and the minority groups etc.
4. The relationship between Indian media and the government has seen many ups and downs the lowest point being the emergency. The balance between national interest and media freedom has always shaped this relationship. The dynamics of Indian democracy has thrown challenges raised issues which the media needs to respond to.

Challenges and Issues

1. *Technique of Production and management vis-à-vis content and*

thinking: Indian media has made considerable progress in updating technique of production and management. However there seem to be little change in their contents and thinking. Naipaul comments 'Indian media have a limited vision and there is an absence of inquiry, the absence of what may be called human interest. Indian media is out-of-touch with Indian reality. In fact it has become a part of Indian anarchy. It reported speeches and more speeches, it reduced India to its various legislative chambers, and it turned into national figures those politicians who were least predictable'.

2. *Growing commercialization of all dimensions of media in this era of globalization, privatization and liberalization:* This has created a dichotomy between media ethics and revenue generation. TRP and advertisement revenue vs. quality programs. Media is treated as a commercial enterprise and hence the romance and passion of journalism is gradually vanishing. Even the press commission observed 'it appears to us that a very significant part of the press and media is controlled by persons having strong links with other business and industries. When media is controlled by other big business they become vehicles of expressions of the ideology of their owners and the selection, presentation and display of news would be dictated by that ideology. The media industry in their hands becomes cultural and financial arm of other business and industries. Consequently they take a vested interest in maintaining the socio-economic interest.

3. *Declining Professionalism:* Arun Shourie observes that 'many of us have incestuous relation with other subjects – in particular with government authorities. Many have cavalier attitude towards facts, many are too lazy to inform them of the laws that image on their work- so many are too lazy to examine the allegations they purvey.'

4. *Accuracy is no more the most elementary component in journalism:* No journalist regards in accuracy either inadvertent or deliberate as good thing but never the less, many journalists condone it as a necessary evil in the attainment of speed and the maximum of news interest.

5. *Events get more coverage than the process:* News must include not only the events but also the process. Flood could be an event but 'flood control' is a process. There is tendency to sensationalize the event overlooking the process which is an important. Media in India needs to serve as a social analyst and educator, thus playing a vital role in the national and international struggle to promote human progress. This is what we call 'Development Journalism', which has not been very popular with Indian media, however development journalism can bring a qualitative change in the attitude of Indian media.
6. *I know, what is good for the country syndrome:* This syndrome is not peculiar to the politician and high official only. The media in India suffer from it too except that politician in power can suppress a paper or channel while an editor at best can only work at overthrowing a minister.
7. *Is Indian media making peace with violence:* too much exposure to violence in media has systematically desensitized the people to violence? They are becoming too casual about brutality. We need a rethinking on this issue.

Impact of media in indian society:

Media' impact on indian society can be judged from three perspectives i.e., social, economic and political.

Social impact: Generating awareness of the people on various social evils like dowry, female foeticide and infanticide etc had led to the decline in the incidence of them. Bringing into focus on atrocities faced by weaker sections of the society. This has bought in a sense of security to the weaker sections. Majority groups fear to do any harm to them in the long run this will bring peace and tranquility among communities. Generating awreness on good practices like health, hygiene, nutrition etc there by improving the living standards. Media is responsible for the success of green revolution in India during 1960s by popularising the usage of high yielding varieties, fertilisers, pesticides and other farm management techniques. Green revolution has improved the living standard of poor by enabling their incomes. Many new enterpreneurs from weaker sections of the society emerged. This has enabled them to rise in the social ladder and stay on par with the so called upper castes. Media also responsible for generating pan India identity and enabling people to loosen their parochial and narrower identities. It must be showing in new employment opportunities that are available in the market, this has enabled a common man with requist skills to grab them. In addition to the above, the media is not only responsible for sensiting our administrators on various issues but also responsible for spreading in latest fashion vis-à-vis dressing style, cosmetics, hair style etc.

Economic impact: media is directly responsible for providing employment opportunities and thereby increasing the living standard of the people as well as spread awareness of a new product launched by a company through advertisements and product reviews, this will increase the demand of industrial goods and services thereby promoting industrialisation and increasing the Goss Domestic Production.

Political impact: media has been bringing out corrupt practices practised by our political leaders. This has enabled people to make more rational choices when electing their representatives and it has also been a major force in mobilising people during elections.

Indian journalism is today more than two centuries old. It has come a long way from the two page scandal sheet of James August Hicky which passed for a news paper in 1780 and which introduced an essentially western media into India. Media in India is the rich inheritors of glorious traditions of dedicated journalism commitment and patriotism. While concluding it will be relevant to quote N. Ram 'journalism in India has major strengths and resources, physical and intellectual at its command needs an internal accountability to higher intellectual and ethical standards, a more precise and less breathless style of work, and public advocacy of its role as a vital part of striving for a democratic, just society. It is very much in need of a coherent theoretical framework to justify or checkout its high moral ground claim, some kind of critical theory of an independent and pluralistic media in relation to the struggle for society'.

3

Media Technology and Learning

The rapid advances of technology in literally every field, including communication, medicine, transportation, agriculture, aerospace and energy have tremendously increased the amount of data and information at our fingertips. As we strive to make sense of unimaginably large volumes of data, visualization has become increasingly important. All these only possible with bless of media technology and learning methodology. Students using well-designed combinations of visuals and text learn more than students who only use text which is the perfect benefit of media learning.

Media technologies have affected every aspect of human activity and have a potential role to play in the field of education and training, specially, in distance education to transform it into an innovative form of experience. Contribution of communication technology has become within a very short time one of the basic building blocks of modern society. Many countries now regard understanding communication technology and mastering the basic skills and concepts of information transmission as part of the core of education, alongside reading, writing and numeracy. The mass media are fundamental to development. They enable people to learn about issues and make their voices heard. They can exert a powerful influence, for good or for bad. Free independent media are important to ensure freedom of speech. Promote democracy, good governance, peace and human rights.

Media technologies are the result of knowledge explosion. These include hardware and software technologies and facilitate teaching learning process. Using media technologies learners are now able to participate in learning communities throughout the world. They are independent and free in choice of their programmers of study and access to the resources. They may learn collaboratively, share information, exchange their learning experiences and work through cooperative activities in virtual learning communities.

By media technology we mean advancement of information technology like internet, broadband, hotline and convergence of technology. Development of the technology undoubtedly expedites communication process and activates media machinery in 21st century. IT advancement has proved that communication has no boundary across the globe. It has also given a boost to learning about happenings and changes in and around us.

Information is power. Digitalization is the only way to access easily access information and communication. With improvement of digital technology, information dissemination is getting wider space to reach its audience. In addition, emergence of satellite technology and digital evaluation have impacted media content and given ample opportunity not only for entertainment programme but in diverse field. More young communities are inclining towards entertainment and glamorous opportunity.

In the era of new information age, our economy reflects growth because of technological advances primarily the technologies of the information or communications technologies. These are like, computers, satellites, video cassette recorders, cable systems, digital audio recorders, compact disks, laser disks etc these devices have had a revolutionary impact on the media. Through all these communication technologies, media gives shapes to the society. However, the technical and social convergence brought about as a result of developments in technology is already creating interaction problems in particular in the younger users.

One of the key issues that have arisen from youth culture and new technologies is the growing dependency of such technologies as the internet among the youth of society. Arguments have arisen over the addiction and over reliance some youths have towards new technologies especially the internet and the various online communities it provides, particularly online chatting and online gaming programs. Among the issues that have been addressed are the adverse impacts of cyberspace addiction, and the displacement between reality and virtual reality and its impacts on real world social relationship, health and communication skills.

New media technologies are set to replace demands of traditional Medias. These are increasingly becoming more than just a simple way to pass the time. In fact, some academics suggest that technology is at the very cultural heart of the current generation of young people. Technology, such as the internet, mobile phones, PDA's and iPods to name a bare few, provide young people with unlimited access to opportunity. It has revolutionized the way we communicate and interact with each other. Technology generates opportunities new things to explain, new ways of expression, and new media of communications and create new forms of destruction.

New technologies have over time branched into the various spheres in society and have been implicated within the educational systems of many nations. The development of technologies and the innovation of communication tools have enhanced various learning aspects. Advancements in particular ICT's have improved the standards of vocational education and distance education for youth within various sections of the globe. This advancement of technology facilitates the pace of development.

Constructivist Theory of Learning

Now-a-days constructivist learning theory is gradually gaining the same respect and attention long accorded to behavioural learning theory. Constructivism concerns the process of how students create meaning and knowledge in the world as well as the results of the constructive process. How students construct knowledge depends upon what they already know, their previous experiences, how they have organized those experiences into knowledge structures such as schema and mental models and the beliefs they use to interpret the objects and events they encounter in the world. Cognitive tools help learners organize, restructure and represent what they know. For constructivists, the ultimate nature of reality does not matter as much as its local nature, i.e., learners' unique and shared constructions of reality. According to constructivism, a teacher cannot map his/her own interpretations of the world onto learners because they do not share a set of common experiences and interpretations.

Learners are able to comprehend a verity of interpretations

and to use them in arriving at their own unique interpretations of the world. The mind filters input from the world in making its interpretations and therefore each learner conceives of the external world somewhat differently. Whereas instructor emphasize the transmission of standardized interpretations of the world by teachers and the educational media and technology they use as well as standardized assessments to test the degree to which students' understandings match accepted interpretations constructivists seek to create learning environments wherein learners use cognitive tools to help themselves construct their own knowledge representations. Cognitive tools and the goals, tasks, pedagogies, resources and human collaboration integral to their use enable learners to engage inactive, mindful and purposeful interpretation and reflection.

Learners themselves as Designers

The process of designing instructional materials enables instructional designers to understand content much more deeply than the students whose thinking will be constrained and controlled by the very materials they are developing. It follows that empowering learners to design and produce their own knowledge representations and educational communications can be a powerful learning experience. Langer reminded us of the important of mindfulness in learning. Students learn and retain the most from thinking in meaningful ways. Representing knowledge is a mindfully task that can be enabled by cognitive tools such as multimedia construction software or electronic spreadsheets. Cognitive tools require students to think in meaningful ways about how to use an application's capabilities and features to represent what they know. Students not only learn deeply and mindfully with cognitive tools, their opportunities for reflection are also enhanced. There is considerable evidence that reflective thinking is under-utilized in education by teachers and their students, a problem that cognitive told may help to ameliorate.

Effective learning through Technology

Salomon et al. describe the distinction between the effects of learning with and of technology as'first, we distinguish between two kinds of cognitive effects: effects with technology obtained during intellectual partnership with it, and the effects of it in terms of the transferable cognitive residue that this partnership leaves behind in the form of better mastery of skills and strategies'. Cognitive tools are important in both respects. Salomon et al. maintain that 'cognitive effects with computer tools greatly depend on the mindfully engagement of learner in the tasks afforded by these tools', and that educators should empower learners with cognitive tools and assess their abilities in conjunction with the use of these tools. Such a development will entail a new conception of ability as an intellectual partnership between learners and the tools they use. Although some worry that this partnership makes learners too dependent upon the technology, many performances are meaningless without the technologies which enable them. Allowing students to demonstrate learning in collaboration with cognitive tools may be attacked by parties invested in existing assessment systems. However, who would assess the ability of an artist without allowing the use of brushes, paint and other media.

Intelligent technologies become as ubiquitous as pencil and paper and we are not there yet by a long shot how a person functions away from intelligent technologies must be considered. Moreover, even if computer technology became as ubiquitous as the pencil, students will still face an infinite number of problems to solve new kinds of knowledge to mentally construct and decisions to make for which no intelligent technology would be available or accessible. Cognitive tools are learner-controlled, not teacher-controlled or technology-driven. For example, when students build databases, they are also constructing their own conceptualization of the organization of a domain of knowledge. Cognitive tools are intended to be used by students to represent knowledge and solve problems while pursuing investigations that are relevant to their own lives. These investigations are ideally situated within a constructivist learning environment. Cognitive tools won't be effective when used to support teacher-controlled tasks alone.

Design of Media Technology for Education

Depending upon the talent, resources and timelines availability for the development effort media technology is designed. There are numerous scientific principles to guide design but every instructional development effort involves large amounts of creativity and hard work. There are no comprehensive or infallible instructional design formulas. In fact, the design of media and technology for education retains as many aspects of a craft as it does a science. Evaluation has an especially important role in the instructional design process, but it is often underutilized. Implementation at the local level is as important as instructional design. In most instances, the conditions under which students actually experience and use media and technology in schools are decided within the confines of single classrooms by individual teachers. While some educational technologists have recommended that media and technology innovations should be 'teacher-proof' to ensure fidelity in implementation, teacher empowerment is more likely to have positive effects than attempts to limit the prerogatives of teachers to implement media and technology as they wish.

Teachers had to make significant changes in their classroom management styles, giving up more control to technology and students. This also changed slowly. Initially, media and technology were primarily used within the context of traditional pedagogical methods and most teachers required years of experience before they adopted more innovative strategies such as project-based learning. Finally, teachers struggled with fundamental incongruities between traditional assessment measures and the kinds of learning occurring in their classrooms. In fact, assessment problems proved to be the most resistant to solutions and many remained unresolved.

The bottom line of the project is that pedagogical innovations and positive learning results do eventually emerge from the infusion of media and technology into schools, but the process takes longer than most people imagine. Educational administrators who imagine that a summer workshop or after school seminars by consultants will enable teachers to implement media and technology in their classrooms are mistaken. Huge investments in time and support for teachers will be especially critical if the adoption of constructivist pedagogies accompany the infusion of media and technology.

Research on Media and their Application

Communication research plays a pivotal role during the pre and post policy formulation period. It connects the idea of development from the government to the people. Communication research on media inputs and programme warrants research and public opinion whenever any programme becomes a subject of controversy or debatable. Many a time people have objected media contents and special programme like Rahul Dilhania i.e., Jayega, Rakhi Sawant's swayambar, screened in NDTV imagine as well as Rodish programme of MTV channel. These women centric reality shows have become objectionable and debated by many feminists and activists. Visuals shown on FTV are often highlights nudity of women and portray unfair parts of women body. Women are used as objects of showing sensuous appeal. In reply to National Commission for Women's interference, the programme makers of NDTV replied women are voluntarily participating in Rahul Dulhhania Lejayage. They never force women or group up girls to play roles in making of the programme.

According to media survey reports, demand for the programme is on increase especially attracts youth and influences their life style. Youth viewers have never criticized the programme. Market research on different youth based programme like employment opportunity, career programme, serials, reality shows and fashion shows etc are conducted after each episode. Commercialization of programme and special issues on youth attracts much and continues depending on market research and communication research scholars. Many debate on depiction of nudity of women have become a regular practice in media in special issues and special stories from local to metro media. The trend is visibly more in metro media in regular basis and colourfully. Circulation is high among youth viewers and readers, according to media houses. It is not media which highlights, but voluntary offer of bolly-wood actors and actress for publication in largest daily matters a lot. Though media's commercial interests are there but self regulation is beyond control.

Ministry of Information & Broadcasting and NCW observed

in many cases be it proactive or sex appeal publications or programme should be screened keeping in mind on social decency. Awareness, self regulation and Law are required to check objectionable scenes and photos before final release. In the wake of controversy and resistance movement, research on media inputs is conducted. As MTV shows on youth culture was restricted after showing for many days. Subsequently media personnel introduced reality shows with participation of popular actors who are crowd pullers and media pullers in western countries and later influenced east audience.

Communication experts and media professionals always stress on one key point 'media literacy for the youth', which has become a necessary amid diversions in changing times. In order to transform social and economic institutions, media literacy is a must. Absence of media literacy one cannot efficiently make out media highlights and research outcomes. Since media now affects and motivates public opinion and life style, so relevance and importance of media literacy be given on priority basis.

After research, the New Indian Express had to change Youth Express magazines and came out with alternative colourful magazine like E-dex for development of youth potential. Similarly the Asian age had to change its exclusive page on women what was shown 12 years ago. In E-Dex the New Indian Express has given more coverage on promotion of educational and employability skills youth which deserves appreciation. Undoubtedly these are reader's choice especially youth oriented and sharing concern for educated youth.

Media and Human Resource Development

Media has significant contribution to human resource development. Its contribution is as important as other disciplines of knowledge. It is to be noted that media facilitates development of human resources in different sectors. It means, it promotes understanding about social, economic and media literacy to their readers in changing times. Most specifically, different organization has their policy and strategy to development employability skills and look after future career of educated and semi-educated youth in our country. For instance, national largest English daily, Times of India brings out Education Times and the New Indian Express Edex, which gives coverage on promotion of knowledge, skill and attitude. On the other hand, other dailies and channels also provide entertainment exclusively for the youth audience. Similarly, TV channels also broadcast career programme.

For best human resource management and shooting crisis, media gives special coverage and discovers conflict management in companies and organization along with solution. For example, national English Daily the Hindu brings out a special supplement in 'Opportunities' on human resource management in different jobs, crisis in jobs and care and concern for the youth. Apart from these, the fourth pillar of democracy provides a lot of employment opportunities for the young budding journalists and spreads its wings in different sectors excluding media sector. Though the opportunities for journalists in journalism are endless, simultaneously media jobs have become more challenging. Journalists have to compete with the each other for the good coverage, fast and quick coverage for the news or any other event.

As the journalists working in national and international fields are especially knowledge broker in society, there is need of training to increase the investigation as well as analysis capacity. Keeping in mind to develop the standard of professionalism national and international bodies like IPDC and IIMC conducting many training programmes. Even UNESCO's new communication strategy gives high priority to free flow of information at national and international level. In order to increase participation of developing countries in the process of communication, the strategy has given significance to promotion of better balanced dissemination of information through capacity building in community.

Media and Social Networking

Social networking is considered as the development of social values through networking. Here networks are created through internet and called as twitter, face book, linked in also. The uses of social networks in media have doubled pace of dissemination. This is perhaps the boldest campaign ever to have broken on Indian Television screens. Sites like Face book even have the options of social games which are gaining in popularity. Their target audience are young because they understand quickly and edgy instead of straight talk. As the youngsters are most tech savvy generation, public participation in media has increased. Media subsequently is getting feedback through this social network. It gives instant space to send feed back to the sender. It helps media to update its specific issues with the increasing demand. According to communication experts, social media governance is a boon for enriching communication among the media company and the e-readers.

Through social networks, the websites of different news paper and channels build awareness for their valuable contents. It helps to increase the company's visibility in the right areas and trying to stick in the minds of the readers through active interaction on different issues. Journalists are getting space to make strengthen their personal cum professional profile. It helps to get connect with high minded persons with the aim of extracting future benefits such as testimonials, links or recommendations. Networking is a way to build relationships that can be mutually beneficial.

Recently an internet and mobile product company ibibo.com has launched its latest ad campaign like voiceover intones in social gaming. The company is likely to join the bandwagon which will help a brand connect better with its audience barring language borders. To promote this kind of ad, these websites are working with television and radio channels allowing their video jockeys and radio jockeys to use the system to build their own benefits also. These ads are being showcased on youth channels like MTV channel V, UTV, Bindass and on certain shows on star one and Sony.

To sum up the whole issue, I would like to say that youths are stepping stone for nation building from the aspect of technological advancement. According to former president of India Dr. APJ Abdul Kalam, 'youth are ignited minds who must not dream a little'. Youth are playing major role in the changing the social landscape of the nation. They are contributing in transformation of economic, social, cultural, scientific as well as political. To accommodate the spirit of social and economic transformation in the nation, media education should be given utmost priority. Media literacy is yet to get place in the syllabus of higher education studies. Youth must know the history and contemporary impact of the fourth pillar of democracy in nation. Students should know that how government and business sector have utilized the mass media and other policies and practices to create a similar vision for the youth.

Active rules and regulation to safeguard the public against excessive collusive coverage of media need to be formulated. Similarly economic and political leaders must not confine the media movement for the urban development. Unless youth put effort through media to address the social problems like poverty, violence, drug abuse, gender inequality, our nation can not reach at the edge of development by 2010.

There is need of a movement to encourage students to examine additional segments of media culture, such as professional wrestling, Disney, rap music, clothing and cartoons, and come to a rich understanding of how kinds are often pushed by corporate executives to enter the adult world at a younger age. Young children are often forced to confront adult or teenage concerns inmost aspects of today's mass media such as sexuality, violence, explicit language and drug use. For instance, large-scale corporations are marketing images and products to very young children, which force to grapple with issues related to their appearance, weight and significantly with pleasing members of the opposite sex. It is very clear that commercial and material forms of entertainment take precedence over getting involved in spending their time 'working for the public good' or interacting with their peers through creative forms of play, activities that 'develop intellectual freedom and divergent thinking'.

Different scholarship programmes and project work based on contemporary issues in journalism are to be introduced whereby prospective youngsters can be trained. It will boost them to know the mechanism behind development plans and policies and the role of media subsequently. Students should be nudged to take a step back and reflect upon how youths are represented in various mass media outlets, such as on newscasts, in magazines, through advertisements, and in popular culture. It will be helpful to make them known about representations of youths in the corporate media and how corporate executives and politicians use mass media outlets to make consumers and voters view youth as inherently 'violent, dangerous and pathological', and frame them as the 'source of most of society's problems'.

It is imperative that students would understand why there has been such a backlash against youths, and similarly would recognize who ultimately benefits from these jaded characterizations. Simultaneously, promotion of citizen journalism can fill the gap between spirit of professionalism in society. In fact, 3R – Read, Report and Research can make the profession successful. It will definitely invite the hands to come together for an inclusive growth of the nation.

Types of median Education Tools

The tools of media education in the modern ear include Radio, Television, Film, Press, publication and advertising. The new outlook and innovative touch to this system has been created new hopes and aspirations among the youth society which has been integrated through electronics media to make it more lively and in-depth love to give a glaring message to this globalization world. The important mass media tools in our country are as follows:

1. Radio
2. Television
3. C.C.T.V
4. Video cassettes
5. Satellite Instructional Television Experiment Programmes
6. INSAT
7. Multimedia Packages
8. Tap slide presentations
9. Radio vision

10. Telecast
11. Teleconference

Radio

Through in 1927 Radio Broadcast started in India at Bombay and Calcutta, the government of India took them over in 1930 and operated under the name of Indian Broadcasting service. The name of the service changed into All India Radio and in 1957 it was made a separate department which is known as Akashvani. This All India Radio is now under the Ministry of Information and Broadcasting with its cut objectives to create a climate of opinion in which social change can take place with a motive to educate the people and to provide them health entertainment along with education in respects of various things to be involved in this process. In Indian context, efforts are made to use the simpler and more economical technology to meet our country's economic, social, linguistic and geographical requirements. This has tended for the effective utilization of radio for broadcasting educational programmes through out the country. In comparison to Television, Radio is inexpensive. The technology used in Radio is much simpler and prone to flexibility. Radio sets are available to the people in the remote villages and tribal areas in our country to provide more localized and need-based entertainment programmes to mingle them in the streamline of the progress.

Television

Television in India was launched in Delhi 1959 and a number of TV channels like Bombay, Srinagar, Jalandhar, Calcutta, Madras and Lucknow came into existence from 1975. Now Television covers more than 95 per cent of total population of this country where the urban population coverage is more than the rural one. Television was delinked from All India Radio with a new name Doordarshan on 1st April 1976 and started to function as the directorate of the ministry of Information and Broadcasting. By and by the growth of educational television brought a new dimension in the field of education for effective utilization and quality programming. The significant functions of education TV are:

- Training of personnel to design, develop and promote and utilization of education Television.
- Production of prototype programmes.
- Carrying out research and experimentation to taste and improve systems method and materials.
- Providing in information, resource and consultancy services for enhancing efficiency of educational Television system.
- Working as a coordinating agency with other organisations and institutions working in the field.

Video cassettes

Video is a luxury in our country so is colour TV also. However, video has come to a common picture and we shall have to accept it gladly to get the best use of it. The educational learners have accepted the introduction of the video recorders which offer new possibilities for language teaching and learning. The youth mass has appreciated its use to form video clubs, video library and video cassettes-learning societies. The most important reasons for using a Television video are mentioned below:

- Source of information
- Stimulates for discussion
- Instruments of provocation
- Illustrations of specific language items
- Pure entertainment.

These is a common features between video, radio and television as well as there are important differences. As with audio recorders, a video-cassette player in a school gives more flexibility to the teachers in their use of broadcast materials. However, there are far fewer video-cassette machines in schools, although the numbers are rapidly increasing. While the proportion of primary schools with video-cassette machines in Britain doubled from 1980 to 1981, this brought the number up to only 25 per cent and few schools had more than one, which meant that they could not play back and record at the same time. Nearly every secondary school had a video recorder in 1981, but the average number per school was only two, not really enough to give the ease of access and flexibility required in secondary schools. Hayter concluded that an increase in video recording and playback equipment would do more than anything to increase the effectiveness of schools television.

There is a significant increase in using the equipment along with the television, particularly in secondary schools. Nevertheless, there is still not enough equipment yet in schools to justify the transfer of schools television to night-time transmission although, technically, it is easier to record television than radio off-air because of the inbuilt clock on most video. The Inner London Education Authority used to distribute its own programmes and those of the broadcasting organizations, via a cable system at all the schools in its areas. Because of the high cost of renting the lines from the Post Office it closed down its cable service in 1979, since when it has distributed its programmes on video.

There are several reasons for the rapid growth. Machines can be rented for as little as 10 per month, and there are many high street shops and back-street dealers from which video programmes, including feature films, can be hired at little cost. Because many of the broadcast programmes are still of high quality, it is also worth while recording these at home, especially since the range of choice at any one time is limited to four channels in the current absence of widespread cable TV system.

In 1981 eleven per cent of Open University students had access to video recorders in their homes and another eight per cent had easy access to recorders elsewhere. By the end of 1982, twenty per cent of Open University students had access to machines in their home and another 22 per cent convenient accede elsewhere. Video progarammes require different production formats from broadcasts, the design features of audio-cassettes will not always be appropriate for video production. The production requirements of a video programme are much more demanding technically and in terms of manpower. This means that recording of material and its editing is separate from the preparation of the texts to which it relates and makes it more difficult at the design stage to develop the very close integration between text and programme that is possible with audio-cassettes, although careful advance planning and editing of both programme and text can go some way towards this.

Whereas students can easily integrated video programmes and text simultaneously, because they cannot watch video and read the text at the same time taking notes during a video sequence is much more difficult than during an audio sequence and tends to lead to concentration on detail rather than on principles or general points. In practice, this means that video sequences will tend to run for longer without interruption, with interrogation of material taking place segments, with some replay to assist. Particularly where students are having to share equipment – either a machine at a study centre, with other students waiting to use it, or at home, with the television set wanted by the rest of the family. It will be more difficult for students to spend a great deal of time working repeatedly through the cassette. This is less of a problem with audio-cassettes. It is clear that in the next few years there will be scope for a great deal of experiment and innovation to identify suitable video formats for education.

The most important aspect to audio and video is the control over the medium that they offer the learner compared with broadcasts. It is worth looking more carefully at this comparison since it highlights some of the unique characteristics of television, as well as certain weakness of broadcasting as an instructional medium. With either a broadcast programme or a cassette, each individual member of the target audience is sending the same material. No matter how specialised the target audience, each individual will vary in ability to learn from the programs.

Ways of using video

- To exhibit a film.
- To record of air programme from the domestic television channel and play it for the class.
- To record our own programme and play it for the class.

- To record a lecturer given by an export to audience and play it to the class.
- To out the sound off and show short sequences as silent sequences.
- To buy video cassettes available in the market and play them.

When youth workers work with video, they are intended to discover new tricks and new possibilities all the time. Working with video also enhances the potentialities of the worker in term of the content, techniques and flexibilities. The use of video recording has tremendous utilities for the youth mass to develop ideas and materials to support the work they do with it. Some of the important areas are mentioned below:

- Intervenes
- Domestic scenes
- Business scenes
- Social scenes
- Banking, shopping procedures
- Scenes involving high drama
- Usually of a tragic nature
- Crime stories
- Comic situation
- Documentaries
- Fantasy production based on popular myths.
- Recording that demonstrate specific linguistic structures.
- Demonstration, cookery, playing musical instrument discussions.
- Ambiguous situation designated to provoke questioning language.
- Mime to which students watching the recording can add the appropriate language.
- Stories (narrated and acted out).
- News items (read out by students, playing new readers).

- Recording involving toys, objects, sound effects.
- Social fiction programmes.

Satellite Instructional Television Experiment Programmes

For national development and for educating Indian masses living in remote areas, Satellite Instructional Television Experiment was geared up, on July 21st, 1976. Satellites are one of many technologies of current or potential interest to educational technologists and planners. The extent to which satellites will be used depends upon the extent to which educational and communications technology proves responsive to educational needs, the extent to which 'cost-effectiveness' can be demonstrated and the extent to which technology in general finds future use in education. Especially, satellites have the potential for providing relatively low cost educational services. Computer-aided instruction, radio, one-way and talk-back television, library and computer resource sharing etc to large number of people and institutions, provided that economies of scale can be achieved. Such services may prove to be responsive to calls for greater access, individualization and productivity in United States education, as well as the need to extend education and literacy to greater numbers of individuals in developing countries. However, to active this potential suitable organizational arrangements and structures must be devised which respond to the particular educational setting of the country or regions.

Custom of the satellites for communication was first step by radio engineer and science fiction in 1945. With two decades from the radio satellite a series of experiments with low and medium altitude satellites, which required large and complexes earth-stations, the stationary satellite was successfully placed in geo-synchronous orbit. In such an orbit the satellite is some 23,000 miles over the equator and stays in one fixed position relative to points on earth. Three of these satellites in the proper position could bear signals which cover almost the entire surface of the earth. The demonstration of the feasibility of using a stationary satellite in geo-synchronous orbit for communications paved the way for commercial communications satellites.

The satellite technology has reached a point where relatively inexpensive, roof-top type receiving radio and television programs or broadcasts over a wide area from relatively higher-power satellites will be feasible shortly. In recognition of this possibility, in 1971 World administrative Radio Conference was held in Geneva and allocated radio frequencies for a 'broadcasting satellite service' in which signals transmitted or retransmitted by satellites are intended for direct reception by the general public.

Two different classes exist in this service, system allow individual reception by simple receiving units in homes and systems that are designed for community location or through a distribution system covering a limited area. However, it should be pointed out that world Administrative radio conference regulations for broadcasting satellite service do not permit direct reception by non-augmented conventional TV receivers of the type in use today. The applications currently contemplated for communications satellites in education are indeed diverse, reflecting the differences in educational systems and needs of the nations or regions where uses of communications satellites have been proposed. In the United States formal systems of education have been serving large portions of the school-age population and higher education is becoming more widespread with the inception of the community college. The important functions of SITE are:

- To facilitate the approach and conduct of television programme of primary schools.
- To train the teachers for optimum utilization of television programmes in the class room situation.
- To train the resource persons of different states to organize the different training courses for teachers.
- To orient the trainees to do simulation exercises in respect of pre and post telecast and arranging other viewing conditions as the special broadcast are arranged for the training purposes.
- To develop a group of good script writers for young children.

INSAT (Indian National Satellite)

data transmission, nation wide direct television transmission and continuous meteorological earth observation. INSAT television processes two different features: 1. Direct Telecast and 2. National networking using existing terrestrial transmission keeping in mind the objectives of TV services that is to provide support to cover all developmental efforts and their use in the betterment in the life of worker sections of the society particularly in the rural and tribal areas. The role of INSAT in education has assumed greater importance, because of its superior hardware capacities. The INSAT service is insensitive to distance that is remote locations are not cost disadvantage.

Extension like radio and other communication links may be added to ground stations providing flexibilities difficult and terrestrial system. It is recognized that satellite systems are by and large more reliable than terrestrial being reducing remote maintenance problem and operational cost.

Multimedia Packages

Multimedia packages have been developed to initiate an alternative strategy by making use of mass media for in-service teacher education which could cover a large number of teachers simultaneously. In-service teachers training courses in science for primary school teachers by using a multimedia package developed by the centre for educational technology of the National Council of Educational Research and Training represents a major attempt in this direction.

Tap Slide Presentations

Tap slide material are very popular now-a-days. It is useful at all level and suitable for all types of education. It is most suited to introductory type of courses where visuals play a dominant role. It can be used extensively in non-formal education.

Radio Vision

Radio vision is an instruction system in which the subject is presented through two-channels, the audio and the visual. The visuals are presented in the form of charts, slides, projected film strips or models while the explanation is given through recorded narrations. Though mass media is obtained held as producing miracle, it is also though of by meaning in terms of its advantage. The mass media can only modify and guide people but they can not make them interact. The communication is from the communicator to the audience where the audience remains passive. The different problems which create challenges in the field of education for the youth generation are realized as follows:

- Universalisation of primary education.
- Eradication of adult illiteracy.
- Unbalanced distribution of educational opportunities.
- Negligible opportunities of continuing education.
- Substandard formal schooling system.

All the above problems can be solved if mass media are integrated into the total educational system, but in this context state government should provide adequate financial support for organizing audio visual programmes in the school level. Besides RIE, Directorate of TE & SCERT, state universities, teacher training colleges should take initiative for improvisation of media materials. The co-operation of trained personnel's should be available to direct the programme constitute for effective cataloguing, circulation and utilization of the materials in the field of teaching and social environment. However, the revolution in the area of mass media is not probing question rather a burning message for the youth mass, who can improve man's achievements in different fields in a considerable and constructive way, where man is moving rapidly from print media to the machines and software.

4

Impact of Median on Children

Children nowadays have wide choices: many local, national and international programs television channels, thousands of video games and films, radio programs, different newspapers, magazines and even computer games, world-wide web and entertainment on the internet. We need to accept the media, especially television, are a powerful force in children's lives. Children need to feel that the world is a safe place and that people can be trusted. This allows them the freedom to explore their world and approach new experience with curiosity and openness. Children's have to develop a sense that they can affect their world and feelings of inner strength and belief in themselves as competent and capable people. To do this, children have to learn what kind of effects in different situations.

On many children programs the characters display empowerment and efficacy only by using weapons and violence. Using words and wit to solve problems is not often shown. Much of current children's television programs undermine development by failing to provide content that help children develop a sense of empowerment. There are very few characters that serve as role models for achieving positive effects in non-violent ways. The more broadly children approach the question of what it means to be a 'boy' or a 'girl' the more they are likely to develop to their full potential. Children need to be shown that boys and girls can do a wide range of things, many of which are common to both sexes. TV can give children a restricted picture of what it means to be a boy or girl, exaggerating a tendency for stereotyping naturally occurring in young children. The term 'early childhood' generally refers to the years of a child's life from birth to about seven. The central developmental needs in the early childhood years are:

- Playing in a meaning and purposeful manner

- A sense of empowerment and usefulness.
- Developing a sexual characteristics identity.
- Developing a sense of trust and protection.
- The need for autonomy and relationship.
- Understanding how people are alike and different.
- Developing a sense of principles, social systems and responsibility.

Play is a basic to the healthy development and learning of children. Through the process of .play, children can master experiences that may have been scary or difficult for them, they can learn to think creatively, take risks and solve problems. Children need to be in charge of their own play–they need time, space and props to encourage them. Children's are developing idea about morality, justice and how people should treat each other. Children's tendency to divide things up into categories–all good or all bad, all right or all wrong–makes those particularly susceptible to material presented in simple black-and-white terms. Most commercial television programs present one-dimensional characters that are either all good or all bad, which lack the complexity of real human character. Questions of social responsibility and morality are not raised when good characters attack and maim bad ones.

Role of Media on Child Growth

Media can never replacement for children's direct experiences in interacting with the world. It can be providing with the kind of content they need to play. Many themes on commercial television programs are removed from children's experience and understanding. Play becomes merely imitative rather than creative. Single purpose toys marketed along with these shows further the tendency to imitation. Children's television does not help children meet their developmental needs through play. Not only does television cut deeply into play time, it also provides a narrow range of content for children to use in play. One of the most important role of parent can play is that of a 'media educator'. You don't have to be trained teacher to do that. Your comments on programs, your discussions with a child about what they have seen, your expression of your values, your identification of the unrealities of programs and commercials are vital to a child's understanding of what he or she has seen and the development of critical viewing skills. When the television or computer is in the family room, rather than the bedroom you can make the most of the 'teachable moment'.

The contemporary researches shows that children's apprehension's levels have been steadily increasing since the 1950s, and that children's level of anxieties and their frequency of sleep disturbances are significantly related to the amount of television they watch. Children who have been scared by something they have seen on TV right up to bedtime are not a good idea. Children watch TV or a video have been through an emotional experience, and may need time to 'work' it off. Time for a bath, reading a story, or a chat with father or mother, will more effectively prepare children for a good night's sleep.

Children's lack grown-ups experience of the world and so are unable to distinguish between what they see and the likelihood of these events occurring in their own lives may think that when they see the same event over and over again that the event is actually happening over and over again can be made anxious because they think that the events that they see are likely to happen to them. At a young age, they are unable to understand the concept of probability so are not necessarily reassured if you tell them 'it is not likely to happen to us' may become quite fearful if violence in shown in settings with which they are familiar, such as home and families or children and animals.

Terrifying stuff is important for parents and caregivers to remember that television and movies, by their nature, can expose children to frightening images, events and ideas, many of which they would never experience in their whole lives, without such exposure. Children see and interpret film and TV content differently from adults and the impact of scary content can have a quite powerful and lasting impact on children. Exposure to terrifying content can result in short term effects such as intense fear and crying and longer term effects such as sleep disturbance, refusal to be alone concern about being hurt or killed and dependence on unusual bedtime rituals. Long term disabling fears can emerge.

Children may have been exposed to terrifying or violent material on television, film or video. However, the events of September 11 have brought to many people's attention that children can also be traumatized by being exposed to reports and images from frightening world events. For each age group below there are tips for dealing with both kinds of media trauma. Some children will exhibit fear through behaviour not words. Behaviors that could alert you to the fact that they may have been exposed to terrifying material are crying, abnormal fussiness or agitation, sleep disturbance, bed wetting, unusually clingy behaviours and greater than normal sensitivity. At the extreme end, there are documented cases of children being so traumatized by viewing violent material that they have had to receive inpatient psychiatric treatment. If you are with your child at the time that they are exposed to terrifying or violent material, the more immediate your response the better, in the first instance calmly removing them from the situation. Following this or if you become aware that your child is reacting to something they saw while you were not with them, the best overall strategy is to acknowledge their fear and reassure them.

Violence in the media is easily accessible to children. It occurs in cartoons, in news updates in family programs, and in blockbuster movies screened on TV. Many computer games feature violent themes. Trailers for forthcoming programs on TV often contain a collection of the most violent scenes. Parents often feel ambushed by these as they cannot be anticipated. There have been few content analyses done on TV or media for levels of violence. Overseas content analyses, which have some relevance as much of our programming, particularly on commercial TV is from the US, show that children's cartoons carry the most acts of violence. Violence in the media is all pervasive and difficult to avoid. Frequently the violence is glamorized and violent solutions offer the way to be powerful. Mostly the heroes are male and the victims are female, showing who does the violence and to whom it's done. Violence media and products are actively marketed to children and young people. The products themselves are frequently in a classification not recommended for children. There is much cross promotion of violent products, e.g, by fast food chains and cinema links, toys and TV series; toys and cinema films.

The patents arte taken the precautions towards their children is: minimize exposure to programs and products which feature glamorized violence. Minimize exposure to news programs for children less than ten to twelve years. These children are unlikely to understand that it is not likely to happen to you as they don't understand probability. Be a media educator express your views and discuss program content for example talk to children about what would happen if they did those violent things at home.

While there may be many entertaining experiences for children to be had on TV, with video and with computers, it is important to keep in mind what children of different ages need for healthy development. It is important that children have time to be in the real world, and to build strong bonds with real caring people. Media can be a thief of children's time that they really need for other experiences–active physical play and 'ads on activities of all kinds. Children need experiences that enhance their development, and all too frequently media content can reduce the impact of programs and games where harmful messages are constantly repeated.

Advertising directed to children includes paid advertisements or commercials that appear in TV programs specifically made for children or in other programs for children and where the product is principally of interest to children under the age of ten years. The amount of advertising can be high as 15 minutes per hour. Sometimes, the descriptions of prizes for a competition or the demonstration of a product in a cartoon program can be construed as advertising. Such practices should occur in discrete segments within the program. Pay TV also carries advertising directed to children, but at a lower level of minutes per hour. Advertising directed to children also occurs on the Internet e.g., in banner ads. Advertising to children is an unfair practice. Hit works by making you unhappy with lives, anxious and unsatisfied. It sells to them by damaging their mental health. The messages for food ads on

TV are encouraging children to the view that what's good to eat is 'good for them'. I fact, television food ads during children's viewing times disproportionately promote foods of low nutritional value-foods high in fat, sugar or salt. The largest categories of foods advertised tend to be chocolate and confectionery, fast food restaurants and sweetened breakfast cereals.

Toys are promoted very heavily to children through a wide range of media. They are presented in such a way as to make them look very attractive and great fun to play with. The children shown playing with them is cute, petty or cool. Toys are promoted on television, by promotional segments within television programs, spin-offs from movies, and links with fast food chains. Other methods include 'virus marketing'. The parents must minimize young children's exposure to commercial media, build a selection of non-toy related videos and choose age specific toys that meet children's real play needs.

The impact of using screen media on children's physical health has a number of aspects. These aspects include direct impacts of prolonged use such as: eyestrain, repetitive strain injury and postural problems. There may also for some children be risks relating to: epilepsy and electromagnetic radiation. There are also displacement effects, that is, that computer use can displace involvement in physical activity. In addition, daily hours of commercial TV will include a high level of advertisements for fatty, salty, sugary and fast foods. These can influence children's attitudes in the direction of 'what's good to eat' rather than 'what's good for them'. Children also tend to snack while watching TV. The impact of hours at the TV set and eating frequently advertised foods is contributing to a rising problem of obesity in children.

Computers and video games were first developed in the 1970s. As technology and programming improved games became more accessible to individuals in their own homes and video games are programmes that are designed for recreational use. They can be used on a variety of platforms that is on many different types of machines, systems or devices. Games can be brought or downloaded from the internet. Keep an eye on your child's overall health and wellbeing and take note of your child's reactions after they have been playing computer games. Watch out for sign that your child is becoming addicted to playing computer games. Changes in eating habits, moods, school performance, interaction with friends and involvement in non-computer activities might indicate that a problem is developing.

Media impact on Children Education

Now-a-day's media and technology have been introduced into schools because it is believed that they can have positive effects on teaching and learning. With respect to education, media are the symbol systems that teachers and students use to represent knowledge. Technologies are the tools that allow them to share their knowledge representations with others. Unfortunately, it is common for practitioners and experts alike to confound the meanings of media and technology in education, and they are often used synonymously. The confounding of media with technology is unlikely to go away in popular discourse about education any time soon, but the distinction between media and technology must be clarified as unambiguously as possible if their impact is to be understood.

The important doubt about the impact of media and technology in terms of increasing access to education and reducing the costs of education are especially high on the agendas of politicians and government agencies around the world. In the USA, the Panel of Educational Technology of the President's Committee of Advisors on Science and Technology included as one of its six major tragic recommendations that technology be used to 'ensure equitable, universal accesses. Another part of the same report called for realistic budgeting for technology-related expenditures within schools, nothing that the much-touted return-on-investment for educational technology was a long-term prospect. Another reason for the attention being paid to media and technology in education reflects commercial or corporate interests. Although printed material continues to be 'the dominant medium format in schools', a recent presidential report in the USA recommended that 'at least five percent of all public K-12 educational spending in the United States should earmarked for technology-related expenditures'.

Another reason for focus on media and education stems from sharp disagreements about the value of media and technology in education. Enthusiastic endorsements of new media and technologies in education are easy to find in news reports, political speeches, and other sources. Many of these proclamations seem overly-optimistic if not hyperbolic. Because of the pervasive and potent impact of hyper learning technology, we now are experiencing the turbulent advent of an economic and social transformation more profound than the industrial revolution. The same technology that is transforming work offers new learning systems to solve the problems it creates. In the wake of the hyper learning revolution, the technology called 'school' and the social institution commonly though of as 'education' will be as obsolete and ultimately extinct as the dinosaurs.

There is no good evidence that most uses of computers significantly improve teaching and learning, yet school districts are cutting programs – music, art, physical education that enrich children's lives to make room for this dubious nostrum and the Obama Administration has embraced the goal of 'computers in every classroom' with credulous and costly enthusiasm.

There are two major approached to using media and technology in schools, students can learn from media and technology and they can learn with media and technology. Learning from media and technology is often referred to in terms such as instructional television computer-based instruction, or integrated learning systems. Learning with technology, less widespread than the from approach, is referred to in terms such as cognitive tools and constructivist learning environments. Regardless of the approach, media and technology have been introduced into schools because it is believed that they can have positive effects on teaching and learning.

Since the educational television broadcasts began in Iowa in 1933, there have been decades of research focused on the educational effects of television in schools and society as a whole persist. A review of the television research literature however, indicates that such claims are largely based upon subjective observations rather than theory-guided investigations, and there is no conclusive evidence that television stultifies the mind. There is also no consistent evidence that television increases either hyperactivity or passivity in children. Another popular belief is that television viewing is detrimental to the academic achievement of school-age children and teens. While some studies have reported a negative correlation between the amount of television viewing and scholastic performance, such statistic are susceptible to misinterpretations because of intervening variables such as intelligence and socioeconomic status.

The most positive research news about learning from television can be found in the classroom where 40 years of research show positive effects on learning from television programs that are explicitly produced and used for instructional purposes. In addition, most studies show that there are no significant differences in effectiveness between live teacher presentations and video of teacher presentation. There is strong evidence that television is used most effectively when it is intentionally designed for education and when teachers are involved in its selection, utilization and integration into the curriculum. In the past, the biggest barrier to the integration of television programs into the classroom was the fixed limitation of instructional broadcasts, but the wide-spread availability of video cassette recorders has provided teachers with the ease-of-use and flexibility they require. Unfortunately, there is a paucity of developmental research focused on how teachers might best use television in the classroom to enhance academic achievement. We know that motivation is an important factor in gaining the most from any educational experience, but we don't know how teachers can effectively motivate students to attend to educational television. We know that feedback concerning the message received from television is important but we lack clear directions as to when and how teacher should provide that feedback and even when recommendations for using television in the classroom do exist, there is little evidence that these guidance's are integral parts of the curriculum in most teacher preparation programs.

The personal computer is the most common interactive technology used as a 'tutor' today. Interactive instruction via personal computer is known by many names and acronyms such as computer-based instruction, integrated learning systems and intelligent tutoring system. The personal computer as a tutor or surrogate instructor has been the subject for much research and evaluation since its development in the late 1970s. Critics of computers as tutors have been around since their inception and there are vocal opponents of computers in classrooms today. The earliest forms of computer-based instruction were heavily influenced by the behavioural psychology of Skinner. These programs were essentially automated forms of programmed instruction. They present information to the students in small segments, required the student to make overt responses to the information as stimulus and provided feedback to the student along with differential branching to other segments of instruction or to drill-and-practice routines. Although this basic behavioural model continues to dominate mainstream educational applications of computers such as integrated learning systems, interactivity in some of today's most innovative applications, such as constructivist learning environments, is based upon advances in cognitive psychology and constructivist pedagogy.

Cognitive tools have around for thousands of years, ever since primitive humans used piles of stones, marks on trees and knots in vines to calculate sums or record events. In the broadest sense, cognitive tools refer to technologies, tangible or intangible that enhance the cognitive powers of human being during thinking, problem-solving and learning. Something as complex as a mathematical formula or as simple as a grocery list can be regarded as a cognitive tool in the sense that each allows humans to 'off-load' memorization or other mental tasks onto an external resource. Today, computer software programs are example of exceptionally powerful cognitive tools also referred to as mind tools. They will be referred to as 'cognitive tools' here. As computers have become more and more common in education, researchers have begun to explore the impact of software as cognitive tools in schools. Computers as cognitive tools represent quite a different approach from media and technology as vehicles for educational communications. Compuer-based cognitive tools have been intentionally adapted or developed to function as intellectual partners to enable and facilitate critical thinking and higher order learning.

In recent years, learning theory has gone through what can be called a 'paradigm shift'. Constructivist learning theory is gradually gaining the same respect and attention long accorded to behavioural learning theory. Constructivism concerns the process of how students create meaning and knowledge in the world as well as the results of the constructive process. How students construct knowledge depends upon what they already know, their previous experiences, how they have organized those experiences into knowledge structures such as schema and mental models, and the beliefs they use to interpret the objects and events they encounter in the world. Cognitive tools help learners organize, restructure and represent what they know.

Following the maxim that the surest way to learn something is to teach it to others, the process of designing instructional materials enables instructional designers to understand content much more deeply than the students whose thinking will be constrained and controlled by the very materials they are developing. It follows that empowering learners to design and produce their own knowledge representations and educational communications can be powerful learning experience. Langer reminded us of the importance of mindfulness in learning. Students learn and retain the most from thinking in meaningful ways. Representing knowledge is a mindful task that can be enabled by cognitive tools such as multimedia construction software or electronic spreadsheets.

Teachers had to make significant changes in their classroom managements styles, giving up more control to technology and students. This also changed slowly. Initially, media and technology were primarily used within the context of traditional pedagogical methods and most teachers required years of experience before they adopted more innovative strategies such as project-based learning. Finally, teachers struggled with fundamental incongruities between traditional assessment measures and the kinds of learning occurring in their classrooms. In fact, assessment problems proved to be the most resistant to solutions and many remained unresolved.

Children and the Internet

Most children art stage will use the internet. Many parents, on other hand, have had little or no exposure. As a result, parents often find it difficult to understand the issues involved and therefore have problems discussing them with their children. The internet is a massive network of computers from around the world all connected by cable and satellite. When users are connected to the internet, they can receive text, images, video and sound on their computer from computers anywhere in the world. Just as there is a book or magazine on nearly every subject in local libraries, bookshops or newsagents, so is there information on virtually every subject on the internet. The internet is sometimes called the world side web. Being on the internet is called being on-line. Playing on the internet or hunting for information is called 'surfing' the net.

Any individual or organisation can create a 'website' on which they can provide any information they choose to. Information on a website is usually separated in a logical way into 'web pages'. These can provides information about a company and its services, promotional materials, information on any topic, reports facts and figures, links to other relevant websites and so on. Once you have gone to a particular website, you will often find links to other websites. In this way you can jump between many websites to look for the information you want. Searching for information by going from one website to another is known as surfing.

Email is an electronic form of sending a letter to another person. You can attach documents and photos which arrive at their destination in the same format as you send them. Email is a very quick and cheap means of communicating and is very widely used.

Your ISP will set up an email address for you when you join up with them. The internet can provide children and adults alike with a world of exciting opportunities. It offers: educational games and programs, research information for school projects and business, the opportunity to communicate with people from all around the world, the opportunity to share resources and ideas with people that have the same interests and shopping around the world without leaving your computer.

There are no regulations or controls on the material that is placed on the internet. While there are three million perfectly safe children's sites on the net, children can unexpectedly come across material of a sexual or violent nature, language that is rude the advertising of children's products. Quite innocently they can bring up sites that do not relate to the topic they are looking for, or someone can send them images or messages that are not appropriate. Therefore there are many things on-line that are not suitable for children or that is cause for concern. The main dangers to children are that they may : access inappropriate information, inadvertently from 'friendship' with strangers, be subjected to advertising pressures, risk their personal health through excessive use and endanger their privacy by revealing person details about themselves, such as their name and address.

The parents are must taken several things at the time of using internet by the children. Being a parent must do to help counteract the dangers of the internet while allowing your children to use its benefit: learn more about it yourself, be aware of what your children are doing on the internet, establish guidelines about safe internet use, teach your children to be criticall users of the internet, put in place reasonable boundaries, use blocking software or filters and if necessary, lodge complaints. The internet is a useful tool for finding information, for contacting friends by email, and for chatting to others with similar interests. However, the internet is but one means of communication and one source of information among many. This topic outlines a few issues of a general nature that parents and caregivers may like to consider: the child's age and developmental needs, reliability of information accessed, safety

The internet links computers and databases world wide. It provides a most valuable communication system for obtaining information, sending mail and chatting with others with similar interests. However, it is an adult world and as such it can be a dangerous place for children to play because they may: inadvertently access inappropriate information, come into contract with pedophiles, be subjected to invasion of privacy and unsolicited advertising. The internet is a most valuable communication system for obtaining information, sending mail and chatting with other similar interest. However, there are risks with using the internet. Some parents may wish to consider internet filtering software as a method of reducing the risks of their children being exposed to undesirable material on the internet.

There are a number of internet filtering tools that parents can use. However, such tools are not infallible, and must easily achieved when children use a web-connected computer in the family room, and not in their private filtering software are filters, labels and safe zones. Filters are software programs that can be put on your own computer, or can be made available though your internet service provide. They are: block access to web sites, or on keywords or phrases, can stop search engines from searching for unsuitable topics, may block access to newsgroups, chartrooms and email, some can be set ability to shut down creation sites are accessed.

Commenter's also noted several difficulties with employing technology without acceptable use policies to protect children. First, commenter's noted that technology protection measures are not the entire answer. These commenter's emphasized that technology protection measures are most effective when teachers and educational institutions can customize technology and use it in connection with other strategies and tools. As one commenter stated, children need to be trained to think critically and use the internet safely. Technology cannot replace education and judgment. Second, one commenter noted that technology protection measures can give a false sense of protection. This commenter stated that children should be educated to avoid improper content in the same unfiltered environments children experience in their homes, libraries and offices. He argued that filtering provides an inauthentic atmosphere that thwarts teachers' preparing their students to deal with reality. Alternatively, another commenter argued that acceptable use policies that appropriate use policies are a good protection avoid offensive material simply by education. He also contended that time limits imposed by acceptable use policies have not been found to stop the ability of children to access inappropriate material online.

The National Research Council report also discussed several issues relating to acceptable use policies. The Council recommended that these policies should distinguish between adult and children, determine how to measure compliance, avoid overly broad wording and strive to list specific inappropriate behaviour and material, protect against liability, and define a user's rights. The best practices and lessons learned that are set forth above provide valuable information for communities to consider as they develop and implement internet safety policies. Technology protection measures are most effective when teachers and educational institutions can customize technology and use it in connection with other strategies and tools. Educational institutions prefer local decision making that gives leaders the flexibility to select the appropriate technology that fits best with their unique circumstances and to consider non-economic factors that may influence technology selection decisions.

Media violence and children

Now-a-days becoming more and more violent in their day-to-day life. They are becoming so self-centered all are willing to do any illegal activities for their own purpose. James Q. Wilson, who is one of the foremost expert on crime has observed, 'youngsters are shooting at people at a far higher rate than at any time in recent history'. The Centers for Disease Control and Prevention reports that a recent survey showed that some 5.90 per cent of the American high school students surveyed said that they had carried a gun. Equally troubling, that survey also shows that 18 per cent of high school students now carry a knife, razor, firearm or other weapon on a regular basis and nine percent of them take a weapon to school. While recent studies show that the amount of youth violence has started to decline, the Centers for Disease Control warn that 'the prevalence of youth violence and school violence is still unacceptably high'. Countless studies have shown that a steady diet of television, movie, music, video game and internet violence plays a significant acts committed by youth.

American media are exceedingly violent. With television, analysis of programming for 20 years found that over the years, the level of violence in prime-time programming remained at about five violent acts per hour. Like television, the cinemas are full of movies that glamorise bloodshed and violence and one need only listen to popular music radio and stroll down the aisle of almost any computer store to see that the music and video games are similarly afflicted. Not only the media exceedingly violence, they are also ubiquitous. The percentage of households with more than one television set has reached an all-time high of 87 per cent and roughly half per cent of American children have a television set in their room. Forty-six per cent of all homes with children have access to at least one television set, a VCR, home video game equipment and personal computer and 88.70 per cent of such homes have either home video game equipment a personal computer or both.

The majority of the existing social and behavioural science studies, taken together, agree on the following basic points:

- Constant viewing of televised violence has negative effects on human character and attitudes;
- Television violence encourages violent forms of behaviour and influences moral and social values about violence in daily life;
- Children who watch significant amounts o television violence have a greater likelihood of exhibiting later aggressive behaviour;
- Television violence affects viewers of all ages, intellect, socioeconomic levels and both genders; and
- Viewers who watch significant amounts of television violence perceive a meaner world and overestimate the possibility of being a victim of violence.

The young children are also influenced to violence due to

televisions. The researchers have performed longitudinal studies of the impact of television violence on young children as they mature into adults. The researchers describe that boys at age of eight years who had been watching more television violence than other boys grew up to be more aggressive than other boys, and they also grew up to be more aggressive and violent than one would have expected them to be on the basis of how aggressive they were as eight year olds. In respect of girls arrived at a similar conclusion: children who watched more violence behaved more aggressively the next year than those who watched less violence on television and more aggressively than anticipated based on their behaviour the previous year.

Music affects our moods, our attitudes, our emotions and our behaviour. In Plato's Republic, Socrates said that 'musical training is a more potent instrument than any other, because rhythm and harmony find their way into the inward places of the soul, on which they mightily fasten'. We wake to it, dance to it and sometimes cry to it. From infancy it is an integral part of our lives. As virtually any parent with a teenager can attest, music holds an even more special place in the hearts and minds of our young people. Academic studies confirm this wisdom. A Swedish study has found that adolescents who developed an early interest in rock music were more likely to be influenced by their peers and less influenced by their parents than older adolescents. With good reason, then, parents are concerned about the music lyrics their children hear and parents should be concerned. Despite historic, bipartisan remedial legislation by the state and federal governments, it is stunning even to the casual listener how much modern music glorifies acts of violence.

Music video studies are valuable in their own right, but they do not provide information about the effects of exposure to violent lyrics without video. Music videos are much more like other video media in that they can tell a story with graphically violent images, the finding that they produce similar effects is not surprising. Long-term effects accrue via the development of highly accessible knowledge structures and emotional desensitization to violence by well-established social-cognitive leaning and systematic desensitization processes. In brief, each media violence episode constitutes a learning trial in which one rehearses aggressive thoughts and primes aggression-related affects, creating and making chronically accessible hostile attitudes, beliefs, expectations and scripts. Video games often present violence in a glamorized light. Typical games cast players in the role of a shooter, with points scored for each kill. Furthermore, advertising for such games often touts the violent conduct as a selling point – the more graphic and extreme, the better.

5

Role of Media on Transformation of Youth Culture

Youth is the greatest wealth and strength of a nation. The future of a nation lies in the hands of its prosperity. The quality of its youth determines the kind of future, the nation we have. To ensure the bright future for a country there is a need to strengthen and empower the youth. They are the potential energy and considered as powerhouse of a country. It is the youth who brings laurels to their country. The power of youth can be sighted only by mentioning a few names of which every single Indian is proud of such as Sachin Tendulkar, Leander Paes, Mahesh Bhupati, Susmita Sen, Aiswarya Rai, P.T. Usha, Rahul Gandhi, Dillip Tirkey, Abhinav Bindra etc.

Youth in India have their origin in the village based rural environment. For the sake of education, searching for jobs, accompanying empoyed family members, etc migrate to the urban and semi-urban set ups. They are influenced by their peers, seniors, teachers and parents to a great extent both academically, finacially, socially, politically. They are exposed to varieties of information through news papers, books, journals magazines etc in addition to their exposure to electronic mass media, like radio, television, cinema and internet. Since youth is the major force for any country's development, their potential have to be strengthened by applying number of strategies. There is a great need to empower the youth for planning and implementing important activities in industrial, educational and social sectors. The activities of the youth has to be observed and modulated from time to time for building a super structure of the youth culture.

Youth are distinct from adults, more self-aware and subject to peer group rather then parental and adult influences. Looking at their behaviour it can be said that fashions, styles in clothes, music, use of leisure time, travelling, playing in groups, interaction with opposite sex are some of the qualities which they display before children as well as elders. Taking together the above aspects, the general youth look forward and develop habits which ultimately arrive at a new style of living. There is gender variation in youth culture. Boys and girls differ on various aspects of their behaviour for themselves and others. Youth are influence to a great extent by electronic media which are born in advance age of science and technology particularly mass media like radio and television.

History of Youth Culture and Technology

The concept of youth culture and ne technology is a relatively new term, however the rate at which technology has moved into the lives of the young as stated by Seel 'is historically unprecedented'. The growth within this area began in August 1981, when IBM released the IBM personal computers. From here the industry continued to grow with Apple in 1983 releasing 'Lisa' than their latest project. Lisa contained many ground-breaking functions such as mouse, drop down menus, icons, folders, windows and copy and paste abilities among other features. Following the establishment of home PC's the 1980s also bought it the introduction of video games; items which soon to dominate the toy market. Video games were one of the first mediums to combine visuals and active participation for children and youths, as defined by the Wikipedia, they are a form interactive multimedia used as entertainment.

As describe in Steel by 1989 out of 20 of the best selling toys on the market 16 were video games and related things. The next major development following this was the internet, which was established in 1990s. it has been described as the combination of the interactivity of video games, the information of computers and the images. Thus the internet created an entirely new means of social interaction. In countries there are high rates of broadband connectivity many of there are able to play online games together. The players are not physically located in the space, they are often involved in socializing together by connecting domestic spaces and time zones through online gaming communities. These activities can have a large impact on the broader youth culture.

Importance of Youth Culture and Technology

According to Roy Morgan Research all most 80 per cent of Australian aged 14-24 access the internet at least once in a week, more than two-third said they cannot live without a mobile phone and 44 per cent are beloved that the computers and internet have given them more control over their lives. The network generation's trend towards online activities and interactive media has also resulted in a dramatic decline in traditional activities such as newspaper readership. More than half of the Australians aged 18-29 read the newspaper. New media technology is increasingly becoming more than just a simple way to pass the time. In fact, some academics suggest that technology is at the very cultural heart of the current generation of young people. For the new culture, a trip into virtual reality is far more significant than remembering. Technology, such as the internet, mobile phones, PDA's and IPods to name a bare few, provide young people with unlimited access to opportunity. It has revolutionized the way we communicate and interact with each other. Technology generates opportunities, new things to explain, new ways of expression, and new media of communications and creates new forms of destruction.

Young people's access to new technology at home, at school, in the work place even at the local restaurants allows for constant connectivity to the networked world. Youth are plugged into every possible outlet, 100 per cent of the time, partly because they want to be and partly because they need to be competitive and play participatory role in today's world. As youth use the new technologies, they produce the substance of every day and making the meaning of their culture. However, the technical and social convergence brought about us result of developments in technology is already creating interaction problems in particular in the younger users. The implication is that in an arena where the law is largely not applicable, socially agreed upon values and boundaries must be upheld and respected in order for us to make full use of the technology available.

New technology has had an influencing impact within society, affecting the way in which people, largely the young populace, interact, socialize and work. Though since the introduction of new technologies there has been many issues that have arisen by the public and the scholars as to the impact new technology has over youths of society. One of the key issues that have arisen from youth culture and new technology is the growing dependency of such technologies as the internet among the youth of society. Arguments have arisen over the addiction and over reliance some youths have towards new technology especially the internet and the various online communities it provides, particularly online chat and online gaming programs. Among the issues that have been addressed are the adverse impacts of cyberspace addiction and the displacement between reality and virtual reality and its impacts one real world social relationships, health and communication skills. Further more issues have stirred over privacy issues of internet content as well as the unrestricted filtering of information that youths are able to again access to.

New technology has over time branched into the various spheres in society and have been implicated within the educational systems of many nations. The development of technology and the innovation of communication tools have enhanced various learning aspects. Advancements in particular ICT's have improved the standards of vocational education and distance education for youth within various sections of the globe. ICT crept through the side door into education with promises of time saving, efficiency and improvements in learning. Many new technologies can see as a deconstruction of barriers between the physical spaces, as communication technology has enabled users to communicate directly from various sections across the globe. The increase in new technologies has made way for industrial convergence, leading to the deconstruction of local centers of powers, as industries move towards a global market place. This has created several central issues for youths, including the ability to adapt to the emerging technological advancements and the global market place, information can now be obtained from several points and young people must know how to access this information if they are to enter the workplace and communicate effectively. The loss of national identity through youths due to global presence is also another issue raised by academics.

Indian Youth

The period of youth is the most important period of human life. Poets have described it as the spring of life of human being and an important era in the total life span. The proper handling of these stages develops integrated personalities whereas mishandling retards the normal growth. A satisfying completion of each stage enables the individual to deal more successfully with future developmental programs. Youth are supposed to be the most powerful human resources of our country. They constitute a huge magnitude of our population. Again the future world is Indians since India is going to have highest youth population and energetic youth force in the world by 2020. An important segment of the youth population is the adolescents. The adolescents of today are the youths of tomorrow in transition. He is neither treated as a child nor as an adult, he is denied the indulgence accorded to a child or seriousness accorded to an adult. So to understand the young adults or youth, we should know their needs and problems.

Influence of Mass Media

Social gatherings during religious fares, community functions, newspapers, radio, television and internet are important events and elements of the human society which put great impact on persons starting from a primary learner to old and illiterate citizens. Various activities, programmes, reality shows and instructions regarding health and hygiene, discipline etc are some of the components of mass media that influence everybody.

In ancient days there was very little scope for individual to interact with various elements of the environment around him. The effects of seasons particularly summer, spring, winter and rain bring changes in dress, food, sshelther and other lifestyles. More particularly the knowledge about nature of the world, moment of earth, life style of people in different cases, living culture of the people etc. change from time to time. Scientific inventions like radio, television, newspapers etc increase the store house of the individual mind by providing more and more knowledge to the persons concerned. In addition to the general public, the majority of youth in the society are influenced by each of the mass media to a great extent as they are more prone to receive information.

Indian youth from the most dominant ethnic variety of the peer group of the world. They constitute about 34 per cent of the total population of the country. They include a wide spectrum of categories like those in school, out of school, employed, unemployed, married, unmarried, tribal, rural and urban areas. The country can reach untold heights only by harnessing this powerhouse. We need to empower our youth for their better tomorrow. Hence, the foremost way to strengthen our youth is to provide them right kind of education which makes them scientific, logical, open-minded, self-respecting, responsible, honest and patriotic.

Youth psychology and the role of Media

Parenting has often been referred to as life's most difficult job and in recent years it seems as though this job has become increasingly rigorous. Technical development in recent years have given rise to novel opportunities for children and adults to access information. Many of these advancements are aimed specifically at the youth culture. All over the world, the media is extremely influential in shaping the lives of today's youth. Today, given the meteoric rise in the accessibility of new technology, more information is currently available for public consumption than at any other time in history. Children and adolescents are especially impressinable and often creave what Heinz Kohut termed 'Self Objects' in order to help cope with the psychological rigors of youth. This hunger for connection to someone or something that feels bigger than one's self is a normal psychological process. However in tody's media dominated culture, the youth seem especially vulnerable to potentially destructive influences.

A study in 1995 at the University of Maryland Studied the phenomenon of the idealization of celebrities among several cohorts of teen and pre-teen groups including kids ranging from 10-17 years of age. The study produced results indicating that each group evidenced some degree of idolization and modeling behaviour related to the media created celebrities that were included in the study. This psychological phenomenon was termed as 'narcissistic idealism' by Kohut who belived that adolescents engaged in this process in order to compensate for the narcissistic injury of the inevitable failure of one's parents to live up to their child's lofty needs and desires. This widespread infectious nature of the public desire for celebrity seems to be all too acceptable in today's world. Entertainment is a major aspect of the fabric of our culture which was built in the desire to be rich and famous and the need to be entertained. As a culture we devour and consume constant entertainment which seems to be both supplied and created by the media. This hunger for entertainment seems to be most pronounced amongst adolescents who are driven towards the egocentric filling of self object needs.

Thus the media strongly affects youth culture. The media executives are quick to defend their role in youth violence and bullying while selling millions of dollars in ads focused on youth. TV producers, network executives, motion picture companies and others in the media deny any impact of their programs on the attitudes and actions of the youth. Meanwhile they continue to spend millions on special effects and marketing geared to increase appeal to youth markets. While corporations spend millions on market research and advertising to creat products targeted at a youth demographic, the still deny ability to influence youth. If this were true to fact, would NIKE continue to spnd millions every year on product development, marketing and advertising? Would McDonalds still be using cartoon like characters to sell hamburgers? Would music labels be increasing the level of violence and sexual contact in the music geared towards the youth audience? Would liquor companies be using youth oriented activities in their advertising? Of course it works on influencing youth otherwise its ideals advertising would not be a multi billion dollar a year business. If it had no influence MTV wouldon't consultant on spending huge amounts of money to ensure that they are keeping up with the youth culture. Clothing companies are spending millions to get good looking individuals to make plain and boring clothes look appealing to the youth. Youth respond to visual advertising more than other forms. This is due to the fact that the youth want to visualise themselves using the product or service. Even adults are manipulated by these practices.

Positive effects of the Media

Besides the conventional notion that the media that has strayed from its boundaries and is responsible for corrupting the minds of youth, the media still has a host of positive effects on the youth culture. The media has served as a boon to mankind. It has provided us with an exposure to the world outside our cozy homes. It has resulted in an exchange of on a variety of subjects, thereby leading to a global sharing of knowledge. Mass media has given the youth of today, an appropriate platform to voice their opinions on all sorts of social and political issues and share information with one another. The negative influences of media that are the result of an overexposure to it are often talked about. It is true to a certain extent that has affects the society in a negative manner. But, undoubtedly the media has proved as bliss.

A recent psychological research has revealed that the media is responsible for influencing a major part of our daily lives. Media contribute to a transformation in the cultural and social values of the youth. It has a direct impact on the lifestyle of the society because the presuasive nature of the content presented over media influences the thoughts and behaviour of the general public. Media has brought about a major transformation in the way the masses think. It has given them an excellent platform to present themselves before the world and contribute in their own way to the changing world scenario. Thus the media has been responsible in making the world a smaller place to live in.

Mapping Media Effects

The remit of the Byron Review is to address 'the risks to children from the exposure to potentially harmful or inappropriate material on the interest and in video games'. Several general points occur from this. First we need to acknowledge that there might be a range of potential risks here, beyond those that appear most obvious and similarly that harm or what is deemed inappropriate may take many different forms. Secondly, we need to accept that some risks may be unavoidable, and even a valuable part of young people's development. It may be necessary for children to encounter risks if they are to learn ways of dealing with them. Thirdly, we must be recognized that risks and benefits may be difficult to separate and that avoiding risks may also mean avoiding potential benefits. These three issues are considered in turn this media mapping effects.

Defining Negative Effects

Looking across the research literature, one can see that a very wide range of potentially negative effects of media have been identified and disused. These can be including effects relating to:

- Violence including imitation in the form of aggression or antisocial behaviour, desensitization and fear.
- Sexual contents include imitation in the form of promiscuous or unsafe practices, arousal and shock or disgust.
- Advertising in relating to misleading claims as well as consumerist or materialistic attitudes more broadly.
- Inappropriate or unwanted contract with others e.g. in the form of stranger danger or bullying.
- Health i.e., to do with smoking, alcohol and drug-taking.
- Eating behaviour in relation to both obesity and eating disorders
- General personality disorders, such as low self-esteem, identity confusion or alienation.
- Physical effects of excessive use for example RSI type conditions and eyesight problems relating to computers.
- The undermining of children's imagination and free play.
- The physical development of the brain, and disorders such as attention deficit and hyperactivity.
- Sleeping problems and other behavioural difficulties.

- Reduced time for family interaction or relationships with peers.
- Reduced levels of educational achievement or reading more specifically mistaken values, attitudes or benefits for example, in relation to gender or ethnic stereotyping.

This is by no means an exhaustive list and it is worth saying at the outset that some of these claims have been much more systematically investigated in research than others. While some of these effects relating to specific media, other apply more generally and as I have noted many of the same concerns have been carried over from old media into debates around ne media, not always appropriately. The obvious reasons, the amount of research on new media is still quite limited and new media are raising new issues. For example around the targeting children for commercial or sexual exploitation that are very different from those raised by older media. It also important to note that there is quite different types of effects. Some relate to specific areas of media content i.e., sex, violence or advertising, while others seem to be the activity of media use In general i.e., to do with effects on brain development or physical effects. Some relate to what might be called the opportunity costs of media use. That is the notion that media use displaces other, potentially more valuable, activities such as physical exercise, school work or family interaction. Other reflect much broader social concerns or concerns about values e.g., in relation to consumerism or stereotyping. All of these things might be seen as risks to children or indeed as potentially harmful also some of them relate to inappropriate material.

Identity of Youth Culture

Youth has its own identity in every society that disguised it from others. They are not silent spectators of happenings but Endeavour to change events in accordance with their own desires, impulses and aspirations. They watch carefully the cultural contents of society and attempt to interpret them in terms of their impulses and urges. This interpretation leads them to build their own culture and this is precisely what we term as 'Youth Culture'. Generally we accept the age range of 15-35 as youth and perceive themselves as physiologically, psychologically and sociologically different from those who are either younger or older. They are having certain characteristics is as follows:

- Most crucial age between 15 to 35.
- With peak intelligence and stamina.
- Time for achievement and career.
- Period of instability with lack of self-control.
- Parental and peer pressure.
- Misconception due to media exposure.
- Craze for city-life, fashion, style.
- High aspiration for more money with less labour.
- More materialistic than spiritualistic.
- Adult mental and identity development.
- Facing unhealthy cut-throat competition every where.
- Seeking freedom from control of parents.
- Transition from socio-economic dependence to relative independence.
- Entering new world of relationship.
- Emerging sexual feelings and desires.
- Dreams and aspiration of future.
- Curiosity and experimentation due to giant-media.
- Stressful life and living conditions.
- Moving towards westernization and modernization.
- Living with doubts and fears etc.

The total picture of youth culture is not crystal clear and also not obscure. Its consequences are fairly visible through strikes and protest in colleges and universities extremist postures, using unfair means in examination are all about to the culture of protest which has become grained in our youth. The youth of today looks towards the west for their inspiration. They show interest in western music, western fashion and western literature.

But looking at the today's time, we realize that our youth is loosing touch with a sense of right and wrong or good and bad. Perhaps we have failed in our duty of capturing their energy and molding it in the right direction and not helping them in realizing their dreams. Education as a potential and powerful means promote harmonious development of the youth. But the knowledge, information and education received through formal means are not sufficient today for sources like Radio, Television, Newspapers and Computer which contribute for educational development of youth. Those mass-medias are the means through which messages can be communicated to a large section of people and it contribute for their all-round development. During the last three decades, the mass media have undoubtedly played a prodigious role in discovering, debating and supporting the issues related to youth welfare and amelioration.

Impact of Mass Media on Youth Culture

For young people mass media both print and electronic is the most important and powerful medium of instruction, information, education and communication, besides entertainment. With technological revolution in the field of printing and electronics the range of media has grown very rapidly in this generation. Different types of media like the books, newspapers, magazines, films, radio, tapes and television which were familiar to the society of the previous generation, have gone manifold with addition of dozens of cable TV channels, thousands of video and millions of internet sites. In this new incarnation, there has been a new trend in media-media violence.

Culture is what a person cultivates in his living through the process of education and environment given by the society. It is a universal attitude towards life. Culture in literary sense is something ripened and cultivated. Ordinarily, culture implies good conduct, polite behaviour and good taste some consider it a set of social traditions beliefs and customs. Progress in music, dance drama, art, architecture, sculpture etc is considered epitomes of culture. It relates to specific art of living, doing, thinking behaving, talking, using language, readings literature, getting married and the like.

In other words, it refers to the ways of dining, dancing speaking, acting, laughing, behaving,. dealing, looking, dressing and decorating, cultivating, growth expansion and development of man from crude life to a graceful and respectable personality is also called culture.

Youth of present day society have no interest in customs, traditions rather they seek to replace it by values derived from other sources like mass media. Hence the youth are changing character, composition and objectives. With the change in role and status of the youth, a change in attitude, values and beliefs is to be admitted and these attitudes generate new forces which will change the social norms. Youth of today have changed their ideas, values and standards which are different from those of older generation. The students of Indian colleges and universities represent their culture and have their significant role to build nation with the changing ideas and value that have brought in modern society.

Due to single family, young children and adolescents have less scope to spend their time with their families. They spend maximum time in watching TV, exploring the internet web sites, using mobiles phones playing video games etc. from these mass media they gain knowledge. But sometimes due to lack of maturity they grasp so many things in an unrealistic manner; which ultimately affect their personality. Due to conflict and frustration young adolescents and youth of today use some mechanisms like negativism, regression, repression, rationalization, fantasy to defend or escape from conflicts and frustration. Sometimes they also commit suicide. Due to mass use of mass media youth are showing less interest to physical activities like outdoor games, social activities, gardening agriculture etc it makes them lethargic and create health problem. Obesity is a common problem found in most of the young adults.

Media strongly affects youth culture. The media executives are quick to defined their role in youth violence and bullying while selling millions of dollars in ads focused on youth. TV producers, network executives, motion picture companies and others in the media deny any impact of their programs on the attitudes and actions of youth. Meanwhile they continue to spend millions on special effects and marketing geared to increase appeal to youth markets. While corporations spend millions on market research and advertising to create products and campaigns targeted at a youth demographic, they still deny their ability to influence youth. If this were true to fact, would NIKE continue spending millions every year on product development, marketing and advertising? Would McDonalds still be using cartoon like charaters to sell hamburgers? Would music lables be increasing the level of violence and sexual content in the music geared towards the youth audience? The liquor companies are using youth oriented activities in their advertising just to influence the youth generation and as profit the companies getting cores of rupees per year. If it had no influence, MTV would not have consultant on staff spending huge amounts of money to ensure keeping up with youth culture. Clothing companies are spending millions to get youth good looking individuals to make plain and boring clothes look appealing to youth. Youth respond to visual advertising more than other forms. This is due to the fact that youth want to visualize themselves using the product or service.

Now without glorifying further the essence of youth like some nostalgic Victorian poet or an old prostitute, I take a direct plunge to the issue of media and the youth. If beauty is instant, intellectuality is slow. Hence, I request my readers an earnest humility to bear my prejudices and endeavourer with a patient and logical conscious. The media has segregated humanity through its representation and stereotyping of characters. Stereotyping the youth has led them to selfish interests with a totally instrumentalist view of achievement. Representation and stereotyping is all due to political, social and economical advantages and discourses of a particular or a personal group. Such stereotypes help the audience in 'effortless gratification' without any self-involvement or debates, the very anti-democratic and capitalistic methodology of communication. Youth, of its inquisitiveness and the mist is moved within the disguises of ideologies. In the advertising world, a fairness cream promises a dark girl a bright career in the airlines. So, is it that Betty lie in complexion? Are the unbeautiful, ugly useless a subject to mere mockery, ridicule and frustration? Is the distribution of wealth and admiring the nature and art only the privilege of the beauty? At least in India, we have the dark idols – Krishna, Draupadi and Ram Whom were worship and lay our faith upon, not of their mere beauty and dark complexion but of their intelligence, self-control and firm ideologies.

The example of another ad, a banking ad (HSBC) shows a boy turning the angle of a telescope pointed at the Saturn to a girl changing her dress and then finally grinning in triumph. The achievement of tuning in to a sensual excitement caused the loss of some new scientific interests. Is this the message of the ad? The carefree action mocked the perseverance one puts in some honest Endeavour. Well, I must pity the media's poor sense of the youth mentality. We are very much concerned regarding the social responsibilities and duties. The unethical representation of the men folk is that they have nothing better to involve in except ideal gossips, cricket fits and girlfriend tensions. We are made to believe that a pimple or an armpit odour, the natural physiological reactions of puberty and job-hunting respectively, can ruin a relationship.

Moving on to the news section and their interpretation of youth. The youth stories are bound within the periphery of sex, crime and Bollywood 'hot newz'. Sensational news captivates our fantasies, giving call to the latent carnal psychological tastes. It is quite a serious issue of how the media includes or excludes views for their political and economical manipulations. Did the news media ever focus on to the pro-reservation OBC's demands and agitations as passionately as the anti-reservation YFE group? The reason being that Arun Shorie, Rajdeep Sardesi, Parnab Roy, Vir Sanghvi and Prabhu Chawla fo not come from the OBC fraternity. Films lead in the rat race of stereotypes. To avoid the shock therapy and a faster box-office turnout, heroes have to be Prince Charming and the girls have to be Cindrellas. Love is monopolized with the bold and the betutiful. Such constructed and fascinated representations are not fair, as they do not portray the reality. Thus, a youth has noting better to do except flirt his girlfriend or ride macho bikes in the streets. A youth cannot have 'jawani' if he cannot dance in the DJ or doesn't sport Jockey underwear. Mardangi in films is all about aggression, howling, bloodshed and Sunny Deol.

Stereotypes in media have limited our range of imagination and the reality. Positive and negative characters are often the result of such unjust representation. Though, they help in cultivating some general views, the media also need to show the responsible youth. Let not the media range our thoughts with their capitalist models stereotypes gulfs social ties. Media must socialize people into beliefs, roles and behaviours. Let every youth live his life fully, give form to every feeling, expression to every thought, and reality to every dream and not get under the influence of the creeping images of stereotypes. Surely, we shall erase out the maladies of confusion and live out our individualities to its fullest potential, pride and liberty.

In order that the youth may grow up in a conducive atmosphere, a lot of preparation and care has to be taken by the government to see that they are guided properly and grow up in a good setting so that they can become better citizens tomorrow. Thus, the government has a definite role to play in this process. The youth are to be brought up well and they have to be provided with every facility available within their means for a healthy and proper growth. The educational system provided to them has a responsibility to see that they groomed well and are well prepared to meet the challenges that may be posed to them in tomorrow's world.

The Government has evolved a National Youth Policy. Its main objectives are to instill in the youth respect for the principles and values enshrined in our constitution, to promote among them an awareness of our historical and cultural heritage, to help develop in them the qualities of discipline, self-reliance, justice and fair play and to provide the youth with maximum access to education in addition to developing their personality. It also aims at making the youth conscious of international issues and involving them in promoting world peace and just international economic order. The Government has set up the Rajiv Gandhi National institute of Youth Development. Its objectives are training, documentation, research and evaluation and extension work for all youth related activities in the country. It also functions as a research agency and think-tank for youth programmes, policies and implementation strategies, to develop multi-faceted programmes for youth, function as an institute for advanced studies in the field of youth, function as a Centre for documentation, information and publication pertaining to youth development and work as a Resource Centre.

The media has a positive role to play in molding children and youth. This role is not given or authorized by anyone but the media is vested with this role by itself. Media moulds the character of citizens by providing information, education and entertainment to them. Media also acts as the forum for public discussion and debate thus providing an opportunity for citizens to express their ideas and vent their feelings. When it comes to youth, media provides to them not only information but also educates them on various aspects of the society pertaining to their higher studies, moral and spiritual growth and entertainment needs among others.

With the increasing involvement of private sector in the media, particularly the electronic media, which has tremendous influencing power, both positive and negative, the media has to play with restraint and foresight so as to channelize the youth and develop in them the spirit of national pride, respect for India's cultural heritage and responsibility for environmental issues besides social cohesiveness and empowerment of the deprived section of population. In a highly commercial competitive atmosphere, government has to evolve minimum regulatory regime to ward off undesirable elements trying to exploit the passions of youth and the impressionable minds of the children.

Electronic Media

Now-a-days electronic media has emerged as a popular and potential means of social interaction and propagation. The birth of electronic media took place with invention of Radio followed by television. The last century witnessed the tremendous strides made in the electronic technology. The simple telephone of long ago has been joined to sophisticated television sets, computers, stereo music, mobile phones and internet. Channels are sprouting up; FM Radio is coming into its own. The internet is showing signs of a revival. Mobile is emerging, newspapers are proliferating, digital developments in media and telecommunications receive the greatest attention and time is the mixed-media-age.

Radio and Television

The Radio and the Television are two very effective channels through which the masses could be reached. Through the television come all types of news, talk-shows, documentaries and the ubiquitous advertisement, clips. Large number of people is reached daily in this way; people with extraordinary talents, new ideals and dreams are exposed and propagated by the television. The modern life style has been changed due to the extensive use of this mode of communication. But today, violence, crimes, murders, turmoil on television and films also do a lot of harm on the young viewers. Guns, knives, bombs and other type of killing tools were increasingly displayed. The youth of today accepted a hero or heroine as his icon of life. They dress like a movie star, color their hair, drive like them and living a life of unrestrained imitation of what they see on television. It is harmful when they are carried out to extremes that they lose touch with themselves and so live in a fantasy world, reality has little to do with such shows. The educational values of some programmes are unquestionable. Most of the programmes gave us a better perspective of the world we live in the dangers, our heritage and the responsibilities we have etc the various channels keep the youth vigilant and updated. It keeps the inquisitive mind busy and satisfies every intellectual query of a probing mind.

Youth of today with a FM radio in ear and spending hours together before the so-called, idiot-box and become victims of the little 'devil'. Their bodies duffer from physical and mental laziness. No one wants to engage in other more creative activities like conversing, reading or simply sharing together. On the whole, the usefulness of TV as a source of entertainment and recreation is undoubted. But the danger lies in the possibility of addictions to TV. So the use of TV with care will be a boon for youth along with TV. There are other means of electronic media like cinema, internet, which are fast growing and are extremely popular day-by-day.

Films and Advertisements

Enjoying a movie is the most popular means of entertainment for a youth. They watch cinema not only as a means of entertainment but also as an escape from the monotony boredom, anxiety and troubles of life. For them it is a restful, pleasurable and entertaining means of rewarding and relaxing after a long days work. As the most effective means of mass communication cinema has been educative value and it is a very effective reformative instrument. Films on issues like dowry, women education, female feticide, youth unrest, corruption, unemployment, poverty, illiteracy can create social awareness among the youth. But the youth of today are mostly interested on the commercial film than the art films. Film is a great unifying force for the youth. They should not only enjoy the music, dancing but also the script, direction also. Unfortunately, films of today has distracted the youth from the right direction. The culture of crime, violence, murder, terrorism is reflected so powerfully thought this media; the youth face difficulty to keep him aloof from this. They are forgetting to realize the sensible and relevant themes of the films. The average song of the commercial films is replete with vulgar thrusts. Women are depicted through physical attributes on excruciating close up.

Films need not be didactic but they still can pass on constructive messages subtly to the masses. The silver screen spreads and sells not just dreams but captivates the hearts of young boys and girls. Hence, this medium should be used judiciously and wisely and can show right direction to our youth. Used with pure sensibility, this media can help in bringing about positive changes in the youth minds. At present advertisements stare and scream at us from every street corner, every newspaper, every magazine, every hoarding, every stall or shop or showrooms to walls of every public building, vehicle, radio, TV and internet. It has invaded every aspect of our day to day life dealing our conversations, our thoughts, behaviours etc. One has to rely upon advertisements from education to career building, from buying soap to a mobile. Particularly the youth are more biased by those advertisements. They feel that as if nothing can be achieved without advertisements. Advertisements have touched all the aspects of modern complexities and have complicated man's life more. People became more confused than finding any solution to their problems. The ad-medias are playing and encash upon the psychology of youth in order to achieve their ends. It is being seen, these day's advertisements are capturing the minds of youth and then create a whole new tantalizing world of fantasy, glamour and unreality among them. Psychologically, they became confused, restless, dependent etc.

Print-Media

Along with electronic media, the role of print-media has been augmenting day by day. There has been a world-wide growth and circulation of the print-media around the world through the emergence of electronic media and the internet. As a vigilant watching, it has created awareness among the people. They can update themselves just by going through the newspaper, getting news from every corner of the world. All magazines and newspapers have special columns for youth. The youth of today going through the current events can intelligently participate in the political, social and economic affaires of the country. Print-media provides great incentive to every section of people by advertisements on sale, shops, electronic goods, matrimonial, job opportunities etc. On the other side people associated with robberies, thefts, murders, rapes, drugs, alcoholism, terrorism activities are exposed through this media. Sometimes, young people are biased by that news either positively or negatively. People involved in wrong or unethical business know the power and potential of print-media and suppressed themselves.

Many times, the newspapers, books, journals cater to the transient needs of life and appeal to the emotions of masses. Particularly, the youth are easily motivated by communal propaganda and inclined to particular ideology. Their aspiration for earning more money in less time sometimes put them in loss and it becomes extremely disastrous for the society. Hence, an impartial print-media is the need of the hour and it should try to broaden the outlook of present young masses by generating interest and awareness through constructive ideas.

Cell Phones

With high levels of mobile telephone, penetration a mobile culture has evolved. It is very common that every adult own a mobile phone in his pocket. It has become a fashion object with users decorating, customizing and adding different accessories to their mobile phones to reflect their personality. In stead of necessary now it has become a prestige and status symbol especially for young boys and girls. This has given rise to an increase in criminal and unethical activities so that they can get extra money to satisfy this growing need to snob. The youth mass are using it in prohibited places like libraries, schools, colleges, examination halls, assemblies. More over recent research and scientific evidences support that there is a high health risk for its users. Such mobile phones have mostly connected with road accidents. Specifically it is found that people lose their control of the vehicles while talking on the mobile telephones simultaneously while driving. Mobile has been major distracters on roads and is proving to be as harmful as driving under the influence of alcohol. It is also alleged that during the conversation on a mobile people are ignoring the persons sitting besides them. Users often speak at increased volume in a publication, with little regard for other people nearby. Some how that small screen also depict the erotic and sexual exposure of young boys and girls in negative use. All these informative models have great influential to way-ward youth.

Despite all the abuses of cell phones, one can not deny the uses of mobiles. No doubt, it saves a lot of time, energy and increase one-ton-one relationship. The SMS is also a convenient way to keep in touch with many persons and spending a quick message. But unfortunately it is misused. It is a great source of entertainment for youth. They lisen to songs, play games, get live cricket results etc. Every youth should use it in a proper and beneficent manner. All one has to remember that mobiles are invented for our conveniences not to creat nuisance. If used judiciously, wisely, mobile can be of great use.

Internet

The internet has revolutionized the computer and

communications world like nothing before this internet is at once a worldwide broadcasting capacity, a mechanism and interaction. It has a lot of advantages for the current age. People of all ages, colours, creeds and countries freely share ideas, stories, data, opinions and products. A great deal of information is easily available within a fraction of seconds. In the age of '.com' the internet is a boom for youth providing variety of information on employment, education, research, matrimonial, business, industry etc. It is especially good for students providing a powerful economical way to conduct a real job search. The youth of 21st Century has been governed by cyber-world, syber-space and computer cybernetics. Most of them are miss-utilizing this media for entertainment purpose only. Cyber-crimes, chatting, accessing to web on-line has been made fashion for youth. The cybernetic revolution has changed their lifestyle, made of living etc. For a youth of rural it is still a mirage whereas it acts as a miracle for urban.

Problems of the Youth

- Adjustment in home, school, society and to opposite sex.
- Freedom from home.
- Unemployment or vocational problems.
- Occupational adjustments.
- Financial problems.
- Health adjustment.
- Religious conflicts.
- Conflicts with friends and family members.
- Failures.

The media enacted problems of youth will be there, but their attitudes, values, influences and character to be given due attention. Problem areas like corruption, confrontation, divisiveness, communalism, regionalism and intolerance continue to affect the social life of youth. Due to increasing unemployment, we have been unable to keep our youth busy in constructive works. Unless harnessed and tapped in the right way, this very energetic youth can tip over the other side and become destructive and dangerous for the society. Crime and violence will be his life and living. As an agenda for the new century the media should take up the challenge of depicting real images and preparing the growth for a developed nation. The creative potential coupled with their zeal, enthusiasm, energy and versatility can work wonder for the country. Let us focus on constructively using the youth power for the betterment of the nation. Let us aim at empowering our youth for a better future and a brighter tomorrow where goodness is valued and greatness is respected.

The new media technology is something other than a progressive chain of events. The storm of progress blows so hard as to obscure our vision of what is actually happening. What is hyperbolized as revolutionary train of events can be seen as a far more evolutionary and transforming process. Three decades of societal and cultural alignment of digital machinery yielded a host of innovations, trials, failures and problems, accompanied by hype-hopping popular and academic discourse. Meanwhile new media studies crystallized internationally into an established academic discipline. The new media technologies are changing very frequently. They are changing how news is produced by including story telling process. It has revolutionized the day-to-day work of journalists and they provide new opportunities for the young journalist and information scientists to work more efficiently and more professionally. Media in India has to bear in mind that it has to be socially responsible in order to survive and carry on its course of work naturally. Article 19(1)(a) of the Indian Constitution talks about freedom of expression and speech. This covers the freedom of press too. This theoretically means that the media is free to do anything that pleases it. But it is bound by certain limitations and self-imposed moral obligations.

6

Media Impact on Health

Mass media are inttensively employed in public health. Mass media are tools for the transfer of information, concept and idea to both general and specific audiences. They are important tools in advancing public health goals. Communicating about health through mass media is comples, however, and challenges professionals. One of the key functions of mass media is educating in deverse disciplines. The mass media are capable of facilitating short-term, intermediate-term and long-term effects on audiences.

An issue of great importance of public health today is how to mount programs that change behaviour in order to improve the health of our population. Although theats to the public have come from various domains, health behaviour is a primary concern because of its large contribution to morbidity and premature mortality. Therefore, it is very essential to promote health of the people. Health promotion is the process of enabling people to increase control over, and to improve their health. To reach a complete state of physical, mental and social well being an individual or group must be able to identify and realize aspirations, to satisfy needs, and to change or cope with the environment. Health is therefore, as a resource for every day life, not the objective of living. Health is a positive concept emphasizing personal and social resources as well as physical capacities.

Health promotion is just the responsibility of the health sector, but goes beyond healthy life style to well being. Health promotion activities are strongly linked with the social context, among others with the mass media, who is a powerful companion in health promotion actions. Media is widely used as a tool for health promotion. Beside explicit health communication there is also plenty of implicit health information in the media, message which unintentionally and unconsciously are related to health. Talking about heaalth promotion, i.e., health promotion discourse in the media is influenced by cultural determinants, such as societal values, norms and beliefs.

The aim of mass media in health field is to promote health and well being among individuals, communities and populations, enabling them to address the broad determinants of health in order to reduce the vulnerability and risks to ill health, disability throughout the life cycle, especially among poor and marginalized groups and promote human rights, bring social advancement through the use of creative media.

The appropriateness of mass media as a vehicle for health promotion or as generators of health insight is subject to debate. Since the 1970s it has gained increasing popularity as a strategy for delivering preventive health messages. Mass media programs appear to have a number of advantages over traditional public health strategies. On the other hand, the public health community has long been concerned about the mass media as a source of problems. Various types of advertising and the portrayal of health compromising behaviours and products in the media have been identified as promoting disease rather than health. The potential influence of movies, advertising media and television programming has been considered in regard to alcohol, tobacco, violence, nutritional behaviour, sexual behaviour, traffic safety and various other public health threats.

The advantages of mass media programs include the ability to reach a large propotion of the population. Although it is important to bear in mind that a health promotion 'exhibition' will probably only draw in people who are interested, the people who are motivated and most probably not the people who are aware of any need for health promotion. Perhaps more to the points mass media interventions are relatively inexpensive method of exposing the population to health information. The mass media can make use of 'visually potent images' to invent a hard-hitting and powerful message which is more often than not available to other avenues. However, the role of the media in initiating widespread and long-lasting behaviour change may be overrated. The constant mass media support constitute a valuable help in educating people to properly improve their behaviour health problems.

With television programs and even cable channel designed and marketed specifically for babies, whether kids under two years of age should be watched becomes an important question. While we are learning more all the time about early brain development, we do not have a clear idea how television may affect it. Some studies link early TV viewing with later attention problems, such as ADHD. However, some other the exports disagree with these results. One study found that TV viewing before age three slightly hurt several measures of later cognitive development, but that between ages three and five it slightly helped reading scores.

The earlier years are crucial in a development. The Academy is concerned about the impact of television programming intended for children younger than age two and how it could affect your child's development. Pediatricians strongly oppose targeted programming especially when it used to market toys, games, dolls, unhealthy food and other products to toddlers. Any positive effect of television on infrants and toddlers is still open to question, but the benefits of parent-child interactions are proven. Under age two talking singing, reading, listening to music or playing are for more important to a child's development than any TV show. In addition, TV can discourage and replace reding. Reading requires much more thinking than television and we know that reading fosters young people healthy brain development. Kids from families that have TV on a lot spend less time reading and being read to and are less likely to be read.

Literally thousands of studies since 1950s have asked whether there is a link between exposure to media violence and violent behaviour. All but 18 have answered, 'yes'. The evidence from the research is overwhelming. Extensive research evidence indicates that media violence can contribute to aggressive behaviour, be sensitization to violence, nightmares and fear harmed. Watching violence shows is also linked with having less empathy toward others.

Violence in the media, psychogists help protect children from harmful effects. Decades of psychological research confirms that media violence can increase aggression. Desensitizing effects of violence media on helping others this study by a University of Michigan researcher demonstrates that watching violent media can affect willingness to help others in need. Congressional public health summit a statement of the American Academy of Pediatrics, America. Academy of Children & Adolescent Psychiatry, American Psychological Association, American Medical Association, American Academy of Family Physicians, American Psychiatric Association.

Children can come to view the world as a mean and scary place when they take violence and other discribing them on TV to be accurate in real life.

- Symptoms of being frightened or upset by TV stories can include bad dreams, anxious feelings, being afraid of being alone, withdrawing from friends and missing school.
- Fears caused by TV can cause sleep problems in children.
- Scary-looking things like grotesque monsters espicially frighten children aged two to seven. Telling them that the images are not real does not help beçause kids under age eitht cannot always tell the difference between fantasy and reality.
- Many children exposed to scary movies regret that they watch because of intensity of their fright reactions.
- Children ages 8-12 years who view violence are frightened that they may be a victim of voilence or a natural disaster.
- Violence threats shown on TV can cause school-aged kids to feel fright and worry. When the threat is shown as news it create stronger fears than when it is shown as fictional.

Watching the Televison impact on Performance in School

- TV viewing may replace activities that we know help with school performance, such as reading, doing homework, pursuing hobbies and getting enough sleep.
- One research study founded that TV's effects on educational

achievement at age of 16. Watching more TV in childhood increased chances of dropping out of school and decreased chances of getting a college degree, even after controlling for confounding factors.

- Watching TV at age four was one factor found to be associated with bullying in grade school.

TV can affect Children Health

TV is a public health issue in several different ways. First of all, kids get lots of information about health from TV, much of it from ads. Ads do not generally give true or balanced information about healthy lifestyles and food choices. The majority of children who watch health-related commercials believe what the ads say. Second, watching lots of television can lead to childhood obesity and overweight. Finally, TV can promote risky behaviour, such as trying dangerous stunts, substance use and abuse and irresponsible sexual behaviour.

Watch more TV are more likely to be overweight

- University of Michigan researchers found that just being awake and in the room with the TV on more than two hours a day was a risk factor for being overweight at ages three and four-and a half.
- The effects can carry on into adult wight problems. Weekend TV viewing in early childhood affects body mass index or overweight in adulthood.
- University of Michigan researchers and their colleagues who investigated whether diet, physical activity, sedentary behaviour or television viewing predicted body mass index among 3 to 7 years old children, found that physical activity and TV viewing are most associated with overweight risk. TV was a bigger factor than diet. Inactivity and TV became stronger predictors as the children aged.
- Children who watch TV are more likely to be inactive and tend to snack while watching TV.

- Many TV ads encourage unhealthy eating habits. Two-third of the 20,000 TV ads an average child sees each year are for food and most are high-sugar foods. After school TV ads taget children with ads for unhealthy foods and beverages, like fast food and sugary drinks.
- All television shows, even educational non-commercial shows, replace physical activity in your children's life.
- While watching TV, the metabolic rate seems to go even lower than during rest this means that a person would burn fewer calories while watching TV than when just sitting quietly, doing nothing.
- The food and beverage industry targets children with their television marketing, which may include commercials, product placement and character licensing. Most of the products pushed on kids are high in total calories, sugars, salt and fat and low in nutrients.
- Children watching Spanish-language TV after school and in the evening see lots of ads for food and drink. Much of it targets kids and most of the ads are for unhealty foods like sugared drinks and fast food. This advertising may play a role in the high risk of overweight among kids.
- Results from recent studies have reported success in reducing excess weight gain in preadolescents by restricting TV viewing.

Watching TV can cause sleep problems

- Television visin is associated with altered sleep patterns and sleep disorders among children and adolescents.
- Regular sleep schedules are an important part of healthy sleep. A recent study found that infants and toddlers who watch TV have more irregular sleep schedules. More research is needed to find out whether the TV viewing is the cause.
- Those sleep disturbances may persist. Teens who watched three or more hours of TV per day had higher risk of sleep problems by early adulthood.

Attempt to mimic stunts

- Injuries are the leading cause of death in children and watching unsafe behaviour on TV may increase children's risk-taking behaviour.
- Kids have been injured trying to repeat dangerous stunts they have seen on television shows.
- Many kids watch TV sporting news events. Researcher surveyed TV sports event ads to assess what kids might be seeing. Almost half of all commercial breaks during sporting events containing at least on ad that showed unsafe behaviour or violence.

TV viewing may promote alcohol use

- The presence of alcohal on TV runs the gamut from drinking or talking about drinking on prim-time shows, to beer ads, to logos displayed at sporting events.
- Many studies have shown that alcohol drinks are the most common beverage portrayed on TV and that they are almost never shown in a negative light.
- Alcohol has damaging effects on young people's developing brains and the damage can be permanent. TV ads are a major factor in normalising alcohol use in the minds of children, adolescents and college students.
- Ads for alcohol portray people as being happier, sexier and more successful when they drink. Alcohol advertising including TV ads, contrinutes to an increase in drinking among youth.
- Television ads for alcohol such as alcopop which combine that sweet taste of soda pop in a liquor branded malt beverage may target youth especially girls and hispanic and African American kids.
- The center on alcohol marketing and youth at Georgetown University found that in 2003 the top 15 prime time programs most popular with teens all had alcohol ads.
- Alcohol is increasingly advertised during programs that young people are more likely to watch than people of legal drinking age.

Even though tobacco ads are banned on TV, young people still see people smoking on programs and movies shown on television. The tobacco industry uses product placement in films. Smoking in movies increased throughout the 1990s. Internal tobacco industry documents show that the tobacco industry purposefully markets their product to youth. The industry uses subtle strategies like logos at sporting events, product placement and celebrities smoking to get around the ban on TV advertising for their products. Kids who watch more TV start smoking at an earlier age. The relationship between television viewing and age of starting smoking was stronger than that of peer smoking parental smoking and gender. Now the Center for Media Literacy believes in empowerment through education that kids need to learn how to think critically about TV and other media. Media Awareness Network is a Canadian group with a wealth of information for parents. The Center for Screentime Awareness sponsors National TV turn-off week each year. Future TV turn-off weeks are spring and fall: 19-25th April 2010 and September 19-25, 2010. TV turn-off week is supported by over 70 national organisations including the American Medical Association, American Acamdey of Pediatrics, National Education Association and President's Council on Physical Fitness and Sports.

7

Role of Electronic Media

The role of the electronic media in India is promoting the formation of democratic regimes. With the dramatic expansion of various forms of electronic interchange, including electronic mail and the internet opportunities for communication across national boundaries and cross fertilization of ideas are greater than ever before. An attempt here that access to electronic information can have positive impact in promoting democracy by providing civil society with greater leverage vis-à-vis the state and political elites and pros and consequences of electronic media (other than internet, because discussed separate).

The general belief holds that representative government is the form of democracy that is feasible in today's sprawling, heterogeneous nation-sates. However, interactive telecommunications now make it possible for tens of millions of widely dispersed citizens to receive the information they need to carry out the business of government themselves, gain admission to the political realm and retrieve at least some of the power over their own lives and goods that many believe their elected leaders are squandering.

Since the earliest conceptualization and discussion of the political, communication has held an equally prominent position both in terms of its necessary for political ideas to be transmitted and replicated and as a tool by which political actors seek to ensures the predominance of their ideas through improved methods of communication. In the polls, as conceived by Aristotle, direct communication among and between all the political actors in the system was an attainable ideal. The growth of large and more geographically diverse states necessitated the development of alternative modes of interaction as societies moved from direct political interaction to representative political action. Those chosen to represent the interests of others in the political system have historically used a variety of methods to obtain information about their constituents' preferences, including physically touring their districts periodically, reading letters from constituents and polling their constituents about key issues. All these methods can be time consuming and costly to employ, limiting the frequency with which they can be used and by extension the quality of information which can be regularly obtained. However, the changing nature of communication ushered in by the drawing of the age of electronic communications and the concomitant decline in the costs of communication on a global scale has profound implications for political interaction among representatives and their constituents and for economic and political development throughout the world. In this chapter focuses explicitly on the impact these changes have on communication and potentially on the formation and maintenance of democratic system in India.

Media Scenario

As India concluded its celebration of 63 years of independence this year, having initiated a process of economic reform in the early part of the decade, the forces of privatization and globalization have unleashed dramatic changes in the country's media. Admidst a deluge of film-based entertainment, news and current affairs provided by private channels. All India radio and Doordarshan once the country's officially anointed public service broadcasters have become undecided incarnations of their former selves. This time the history of Indian media is critical: it's overwhelming in the quick and dramatic changes over the last few years and frustrating in the current impasse thanks to the imbroglio over the newly instituted Broadcasting Authority of India.

For those in the business of renting eyeballs, the delinking of radio and television from direct state control has given endless joy. But media analysts and NGOs have varied responses. Some of the deregulation of broadcast media is potentially aiding the emergence of community radio and other forms of more democratic, participatory communication. Others despair that Indian audiences have been, to borrow a phrase, amused to death. They observe that market imperatives have already forced the once state-owned AIR and Doordarshan to abdicate their responsibilities, ringing the death knell on the state's role in public service broadcasting. The role has been one of mixed successes. Over the last four decades, the state's forays into development communication, the ruling communication paradigm at that time, have been significant. But then the successes of Satellite Instructional Television Experiment or the Kheda Communications Project are offset by the phenomenal failures of other projects such as PREAL and in the long run, undermined by the vacillating fortunes and commitments of rapidly-changing governments.

Today vastly changed media scenario calls for a recasting of the role of media in promoting pro-social change. This paper discusses the prevailing media tends in India in a historical context, highlights the issues being debated and describes the responses of NGOs and development agencies to the changes and the new opportunities they present. An underlying premise is the need for some of the key stakeholders for social change communication-donor agencies and NGOs to strengthen the linkages between the discourse on media trends and their own investments in communication, whether to promote child rights, HIV/AIDS education, sign fly, women's empowerment or the environment.

BROADCAST MEDIA

Radio

The number of radio stations has increased from 100 in 1990 to 209 in 1997 and the land area covered from 84 per cent to 91 per cent in addition to it many FM radio are established from 2004 to 2009 to cover the maximum area. However, despite its tremendous reach and the fact that it presents the best option for low-cost programming, radio has been treated as a poor relative for over two decades. Listenership has either dropped or reached a plateau. In some cases listenership has raised, although very negligible, in some urban area allotment to private companies on five FM stations. Film and other popular music constitute the main fare of such stations, contributing to an increase in commercial time and revenues from Rs. 527 million in 1991-92 to Rs. 809 million in 1995-96.

Some efforts have been made to use radio for social change, as in the case of the state-support radio rural forums for agricultural communication in the 1960s to promote adult literacy in 1980s. More recently NGOs have helped broadcast programmes on women and legal rights, emergency contraception and tele-serials advocating girls education. But it is clearly a medium waiting for a short-in the arm. A key need in India is for local broadcasting that reflects issues of concern to the community. In this regard, some communication experts believe that an increased and accelerated commercialization of radio will eventually drive down the costs of FM radio sets, thus facilitating local radio. The increasing devolution of political power initiated through the 73rd and 74th amendment to the constitution in 1988-89 has also set a climate conductive for the empowerment of communities and local governance. A key area requiring attention is advocacy for community radio and the provision of training to NGOs and communities to use this medium for articulating their concerns as one Bangalore-based NGO is currently doing.

Television

The number of private television channels has increased from none in 1990 to more than 80 channels in these recent years. Entertainment constitutes about 51 per cent of the total programme content, even though some channels such as Star Plus follow CNN's example in delivering news on the hour, every hour. Certain channels are established exclusively 24 hours news. Some other channels 24 hours for comedy as well as 24 hours songs and other entertainment channels also established.

However, in a bid to give themselves a halo of social responsibility, some channels broadcast programmes with a veneer of public interest, soap that incorporate socially relevant themes such as women's education and empowerment, interactive talk shows on whether smoking should be banned and open forums with government representatives responding to audience queries on human rights abuses or consumer rights. These programmes combine varying degrees of social value with commercial appeal in a competitive market. The open forums, in particular have played an important role in familiarizing the public to the political and legal system and in building a demand for political transparency and accountability.

Another genre, that of the edutainment pro-social soap continues with serials such as Tara with dealt with the life of a strong-willed woman. However, while the first Indian edutainment soap Hum Log (1985) transfixed much of the nation the audiences for subsequent edutainment serials have been comparatively smaller. There is no longer the captive audience of the mid-80s and there are several competing channels and soaps to choose from. These include reruns of long running teleserials of the late 1980s such as Ramayana and the Mahabharata which enjoy cult-like status. An emerging trend and one that also reflects the current programme focus of development agencies is the targeting of specific segments of the audience in particular young adults. Urban middle to upper class youth especially, constitutes a key target group for private channels. Music channels such as MTV and V channel which rank among the top ten favourite channels are popular role models for a young generation.

Cashing in this trend, UNAIDS, India initiated in 1996 collaboration with V channel for an on-air and on-ground campaign for HIV/AIDS. In another effort, the Ford Foundation, India funded BBC training for radio and television producers on reproductive and sexual health. The six project proposals shortlisted for additional funding, all of which target children and youth are in entertainment formats of musicals talk shows and animation.

The usefulness of TV as a source of entertainment, recreation and knowledge is undoubted. But the danger lies in possibility of addiction of our youth to it. In this context Josephson reported that the adolescents those who continue to believe in the reality of TV and to identify with its violent heroes are the ones likely to be more aggressive than their counterparts. Hence the use of TV with proper care can be of immense beneficial for our youth.

Encouraging adolescents and youth to express their opinion and to analyze and question TV contents is a parental strategy that can be adopted to reduce adolescents fear and aggressiveness as well as to improve their critical approach to the medium. One highly influential action parents can take for toddlers in this direction is to examine and regulate their own viewing behaviour since toddlers highly influenced by their parents viewing habits.

It would be a long debate to get into the positivity and negativity of the women characters. Almost all serials are women-documented, and if one leaves the family drama and moves to the more modern soaps, there have been some great one, that have taken up bold themes, uncommon themes and worked on them. Soaps like 'Astitva-Ek Prem Kahani' dealing with a young man falling in love with a much older woman or 'Jassi Jaisi Koi Nahin' where a common ordinary looking girl makes it to the top on basis of her merit, have been some milestones in influencing the youth. 'Jassi Jaisi Koi Nahin' has inspired common looking girls, with no glamour to back them, to stand for themselves and crate their own niche in society definitely a very positive play of psychological interpretation of the human mind.

The fact remain that much ever critics cry themselves hoarse over the portrayal of women and the one sided views presented. The serials will go on. A dedicated audience sits glued to the sets and in order to reward this, star channel (India) came up with the 'Star Parivaar Awards' where viewers are given a choice to create their own family choice, so much of that there was a best 'Star Atithi', who shared the limelight with the hallowed star cast. The awards bring forward the view that soaps are not just limited to the women who stay at home, but also women who are working and who unwind with their daily boost of late night serials. Serials in India, claim to have pulse of their viewers, Balaji Telefilms mainstay Ekta Kapoor is of the idea that her serials are the essence of Indian sense and sensibility and her characters and plots are normal people and normal incidents. Again there is no getting into a debate over this since the majority of viewers swear over the characters and their actions. One thing is for sure, it can be an eyesore for some can hate it, there may be historical debates over them, but soaps are here to stay. They have found their way and embedded themselves into the mindset of millions across the country. If nothing binds to strangers, discussions on soap have brought forth the most animated response. Style statements are being set, progressive or regressive attitudes are being set, and emotions are running wild as characters drip tears or acid. The ball has started rolling.

Research has associated exposure to media violence with a variety of physical and mental health problems for children and adolescents including aggressive behaviour desensitization to violence, fear, depression, nightmares and sleep disturbances. More than 3500 research studies have examined the association between media violence and violent behaviour. But out of which 18 have shown a positive relationship. Consistent and strong association between media exposure and increases in aggression have been found in population-based epidemiologic investigation of violence in American society cross-cultural studies experimental and natural laboratory research and longitudinal studies that show that aggressive behaviour associated with media exposure persists for decades. The strength of the correlation between media violence and aggressive behaviour found on meta-analysis is greater that of calcium intake and bone mass, lead ingestion and lower IQ, condom nonuse and sexually acquired human immunodeficiency virus infection or environmental tobacco smoke and lung cancer association's clinicians accept and on which preventive medicine is based without question.

Parent blaming their young children for excessive and unsuitable TV viewing is a very common syndrome all over the world but at the same time, children appear to be most unhappy about this. Our parents keep on saying, read, read... all the time. They want us to do nothing but study. They don't let us watch TV. We do need some entertainment also. 'Without it studies become dull and uninteresting' said one boy. 'Whenever I watch some programme my mother tells me to go and study. She thinks that I am wasting my time. But while I am reading she may call me to help her in her household work without bothering about my studies. A girl pointed out that 'When I am watching TV she will again tell me to study'. The parents say you will spoiled, if you watch MTV, another boy butted in. These answers are among the few, posted by young boys and girls in the response to a question: Is TV an Idiot Boxes? However, there are always two sides of a coin. If TV has made any bad impact that is due to our misunderstanding of potential of the medium with decide: TV is an Idiot Box or an Intelligent Box?

The concept of youth culture and new technology is relatively new term, however the rate at which technology has moved into the lives of the young is historically unprecedented. Young people today can now communicate to other youths around the world as well as access information from the internet via their mobile phone. At today's historical juncture, media culture has arguably become the most dominant force defining the sense of self, driving our understanding of the 'other and providing symbols, myths and resources' for generating a common culture. Youth culture is poorly understood by the mass media including television and in many cases the lack of connection can lead to disengagement in the educational sector. Media (il)literacy is important for many reasons and a light-hearted treatment of the effect of the mass media in the educational sector can lead to undesirable outcomes. Teacher-educators must use the mass media including Television in their teaching to stimulate reflection and engagement on the part of present and future teachers. We must address various issues pertaining to the use Television by the youth of this generation who has already started listening to radio and the sound television from his/her mother's womb.

Children are influenced by media they learn by observation, imitating and making behaviours their own. Aggressive attitudes and behaviours are learned by imitating observation models. Research has shown that the strongest single correlate with violent behaviour is previous exposure to violence. Because children younger than eight years cannot discriminate between fantasy and reality they are uniquely vulnerable to learning and adopting as reality the circumstances, attitudes and behaviours portrayed by entertainment media. It is not violence itself but the context in which it is portrayed that can make the difference between learning about violence and learning to be violent. Serious explorations of violence in plays like Macbeth and films like saving Private Ryan treat violence as what it is a human behaviour that cause suffering, loss and sadness to victims and perpetrators. In this context, viewers learn the danger and harm of violence by vicariously experiencing its outcomes. Unfortunately, most entertainment violence is used for immediate visceral thrills without portraying any human cost. Sophisticated special effects, with increasingly graphic depictions of mayhem, make virtual violence more believable and appealing. Studies show that the more realistically violence is portrayed, the greater the likelihood that it will be tolerated and learned. Titillating violence in sexual contexts and comic violence are particularly dangerous because they associate positive feelings with hurting others.

In addition to modeling violent behaviour, entertainment media inflate the prevalence of violence in the world, cultivating in viewers the mean world syndrome, a perception of the world as a dangerous place. Fear of being the victim of violence is a strong motivation for some young people to carry a weapon, to be more aggressive to 'get them before they get me'. For some children exposure to media violence leads to anxiety, depression and posttraumatic stress disorder or to sleep disturbances and nightmares. Some defend media violence as an outlet for vicariously releasing hostility in the safety of virtual reality. However, research testing this catharsis hypothesis found that after experiencing media violence, children displayed increased overt aggression because of lowered inhibitions. Numerous studies have shown that the most insidious and potent effect of media violence is to desensitize all of us to real life violence.

Interactive media, such as video games and the internet are so new that there has been little time to assess their influence on children's physical and mental health. Early studies of these rapidly growing and ever more sophisticated types of media indicate that the effects of child-initiated virtual violence may be even more profound than those of passive media, such as television. Experimental studies have shown that after playing video games, young people exhibit measurable decreases in pro-social and helping behaviours and increases in aggressive thoughts and violent retaliation to provocation. Playing violent games has been found to account for a 13 per cent to 22 per cent increase in adolescents' violent behaviour, by comparison, smoking tobacco accounts for 14 per cent of the increase in lung cancer.

Children learn by observing and trying out behavioural scripts. Repeated exposure to violent behavioural scripts can lead to increased feelings of hostility, expectations that others will behave aggressively, desensitization to the pain of others and increased likelihood of interacting and responding to others with violence. Active participation increases effective learning, video games are an ideal environment in which to learn violence. They place the player in the role of the aggressor and reward him or her for successful violent behaviour. Rather than observing part of a violent interaction, video games allow the player to rehearse an entire behavioural script, from provocation to choosing to respond violently to resolution of the conflict. Moreover, video games have been found to be addictive, children and adolescents want to play them for long periods of time to improve their scores and advance to higher levels. Repetition increases their effect. Interpersonal violence, as victim or as perpetrator is now a more prevalent health risk than infections disease, cancer or congenital disorders for children adolescents and young adults.

Recommendations

Given the current scenario and the needs of the development, the following recommendations can be made:

- Develop a regulatory framework that defines public service broadcasting to include not only state-owned media but all non-commercial broadcasting. This would empower non-profit institutions such as universities, community organizations, local bodies and NGOs to participate in development communication. This was suggested in a privately drafted, more holistic, alternative to the current Broadcasting Bill, the Prasar Sewa Bill, which was drawn up by a group of communication and media experts. This draft bill suggests that there should be three streams of broadcasting public service broadcasting funded by the state, market-driven satellite broadcasting including cable, terrestrial and satellite services and community service broadcasting by autonomous citizens groups, universities, trusts and NGOs to make more programmes reflecting local realities. However, the draft bill has not been taken into consideration.

- Media education and literacy to create demand for better need based media stories and programmes.
- Decentralization and provision of training for communities to enable local broadcasting and community media. Putting communication resources in the hands of the community is a sine qua non for participatory communication.
- Sensitization and training of media professionals from print, radio and television in social development issues.
- Strengthening linkages between media trends and communication investments of development organizations.

In the absence of a concerted effort by media analysts, NGOs, Donor agencies and the public to support need-based, socially relevant media, the current waves of, and I borrow a phrase here; the LPG mantra will drown the impulse for a media with a conscience. The oft-cited cliché then of the dichotomy between India and Bharat between the cyber-savvy India elite and the monsoon dependents farmer, will unfortunately ring true.

8

Role of Print Media

Mail is the most democratic form distributions of information. It does not discriminate based on income level, demographics status, geographic position or technology use. It provides something tangible convenient, colourful and occasionally persuasive. Print is a medium that must be physically delivered form the originator to consumer in other words, printing in the age of the web and beyond. From its invention 550 years age, though a renaissance and a reformation, though the industrial and information ages, though competitors such as radio, cinema, television, and even computer networks, paper-based communication has dominated our society and our culture. Print is not one thing – it is many different products and each one has different dynamics in relation to distribution methods.

Print media can be a highly effective tool in marketing your business. Using various types of print media, you can build awareness about your business. Print media, such as articles can build your professional credibility and credit worthy of your business e.g., if you are the author of an article about a topic that is related to your industry, the position you will as expert in your field. When a reader of that print publication reads it, it help to form an opinion on your standing in your industry. 45.23 per cent of the printed products are distributed by mail. Major categories are including periodicals, catalogues, direct mail and transaction materials, whereas 26.15 per cent of print products are distributed through retail locations. Majority of this category are periodicals, books, packaged products and greetings cards. 22.38 per cent of all print is distributed by other methods, such as home delivery and direct-to-business private services and 6.20 per cent of the print products are distributed through non-store newsstands, primarily newspapers, periodicals and some books.

Over the last two decades most of the benefits of print media productivity have been passed back to the print buyer. Commercial printers are selling full-colour print at prices below those for the same product twenty years ago. This has been the result of automated presses, computer-to-plate, and on-or-off-press and advanced digital workflows. Over that same period, even with significant investments in automation, postal costs have increased. Print is a bargain and its record of relentless cost reduction mitigates some of these increases.

Based on the above information, the print media is very close to the public and the people are in a position to afford to utilization of those services. The circulation of the print media by day by day increase even thought there is increasing in the electronic media. The print and electronic media are the direct competitors or supplementary? For convey the news point of view those are the competitors, but for circulation point of view there is no relationship. Suppose even though a common man is having a television and the person who have television, also purchasing the newspaper regularly, so both of them also supplementary.

Given national literacy rate is very low, limited reach of newspapers and magazines and the distinctly urban educated readership profile, the role of print media has been defined more in terms of information dissemination and advocacy. The picture is a lopsided: circulation figures are rapidly increasing advertising revenue, but this is especially true of English publications, which account for 71 per cent of the total and revenue of members of the Indian Newspaper Society. A key feature of these publications, unfortunately, is increasing preponderance of glossy, ad friendly films and TV based reporting. That the sole trendsetter in this increasing corporation of the fourth estate, the Times of India, also ranks 10th among the top selling newspapers in the world, is no coincidence. Given the increasing costs of newsprint production and the pressure of market imperatives, newspaper houses have followed the piper in carrying ad friendly fluff at the cost of more serious development and health reporting. Leading dailies have over the last few years dropped their special sections devoted to development and health. The low literacy rate and production costs have also stymied the possibilities of smaller alternative publications that could potentially reflect the concerns of the development sector.

A newspaper is a regular scheduled publication containing news, information and advertising. By 2008 there were 6580 daily newspapers in the world, selling 395 million copies a day. The worldwide recession of 20008, combined with the rapid growth of web-based alternatives, caused a serious decline in advertising and circulation as many papers closed or sharply cut back operations. General-interest newspapers typically publish stories on local and national political events and personalities, crime, business, entertainment, society and sports. Most traditional papers also feature an editorial page containing editorials written by an editor and columns that express the individual opinions of writers. Other facial appearance includes display and classified advertising, comics and inserts from local merchants.

Print media is anything that is offline that promotes your business. The most common types of print media include newspapers, magazines, newsletters, brochures, pamphlets, advertisements, billboards and signs. Print media is any vehicle that is tangible and can spread the word about your business by gaining the attention of your target audience. The newspaper is typically funded by paid subscriptions and advertising. A wide variety of material has been published in newspapers including editorial opinions, criticism, persuasion and obituaries, entertainment features such as crosswords, Sudoku and horoscopes, weather news, advice, food, education news, job opportunities and other columns, reviews of movies, plays and restaurants, classified ads, display ads, editorial cartoons and comic strips.

Print media in marketing can present itself in several different formats. Two of the more population forms of print media include newspapers and magazines. Essentially, through print media is any type of tangible printed material that contains information of some sort about your business. Print media provides tangible information about your business that a prospect can walk away with items in print help to add credibility to you and your business and seeing your business name in print provides affirmation to existing customers that their decision to be business with you is the right one. For prospects, print media provides your business with a way to communicate with them and get in front of them in an effort to win their business.

History of Print Media

Before invention of newspapers in the early 17th century, official government bulletins were circulated at times in some centralized empires. In ancient Rome, Acta Diurna or government bulletins were made public by Julius Caesar. They were carved in metal or stone and posted in public places. In China, early government prepared news sheets called tipao circulated among count officials during the late Han dynasty i.e., second and third centuries AD. Between 713 and 734, the Kaiyuan Za Bao (Bulletin of the Court) of the Chinese Tang Dynasty published government news, it was handwritten on silk and read by government officials. In 1582 these was the first reference to privately published newssheets in Beijing during late Ming Dynasty.

In early modern Europe was increased cross-border interaction created a rising need for information, which was met by concise handwritten news sheets. In 1556, the government of Venice first published the monthly Notizie scritte, which cost one gazetta. These avvisi were handwritten newsletters and used to convey political, military and economic news quickly and efficiently to Italian cities (1500-1700) sharing some characteristics of news papers though usually not considered true newspapers. However, none of these publications fully met classical criteria for proper newspapers as they were typically not intended for the general public and restricted to a certain range of topics.

The emergence of the new media branch in the 17th century has to be seen in close connection with the spread of the printing press from publishing press derives it name. The German language Relation aller Furnemmen and gendenckwurdigen Historien printed from 1605 onwards by Johann Carolus in Strasbourg is often recognized as the first newspaper. At that time, Strasbourg was a free imperial city in the Holy Roman Empire of the German Nation, the first newspaper of modern Germany was the Avisa, published in 1609 in Wolfenbuttel. Other earlier papers includes: the Dutch Courante Uyt Italien, Duytslandt & Company of 1618 was first to appear in folio-rather than quarto-sie. Amsterdam a center of world trade quickly became home to newspapers in many languages, often before they were published in their own country.

The first English-language newspaper Corrant out of Italy, Germany etc, was published in Amsterdam in 1960. A year and a half later, Corante weekly news from Italy, Germany, Hungary, Poland, Bohemia, France and the Low Country's was published in England by a Nathaniel Butter and Thomas Archer. The first newspaper in France was published in 1631, La Gazette. The first newspaper in Portugal, A Gazeta was published in 1654 in Lisbon. The first Spanish newspaper Gaceta de Madrid was published in 1661.

Post-och Inrikes Tidningar was first published in Sweden in 1645 and is the oldest newspaper still in existence though it now publishes solely online. Opregte Haarlemsche Courant from Haarlem was first published in 1656 is the oldest paper still printed. It was forced to merge with the newspaper Haarlems Dagblad in 1942 when Germany occupied the Netherlands. Since 1942 the Haarlems Dagblad when Germany occupied the Netherlands. Since then the Haarlems Dagblad appears with the subtitle Oprechte Haerlemse Courant 1656 and considers itself to be the oldest newspaper still publishing. Merkuriusz Polski Ordynaryjny was published in Krakow, Poland in 1661. The first successful English daily 'The Daily Courant' was published from 1702 to 1735.

1960 in Boston, Benjamin Harris published Publick Occurrences both Foreign and Domestic. This is considered the first newspaper in the American colonies even though only one edition was published before the paper was suppressed by the government. In 1704 the governor allowed the Boston News Letter to be published and it becomes the first continuously published newspaper in the colonies. Soon after, weekly paper publishing in

New York an Philadelphia began. These early newspapers followed by the British format and were contain four pages. The most news carried from Britain and content depended on the editor's interests. In 1783, the Pennsylvania Evening Post became the first American daily. John Bushell published the Halifax Gazette in 1751 was the first Canadian newspaper.

By the early 19th century many cities in Europe, as well as North and South America published newspaper-type publications through not all them developed in the same way, content was vastly shaped by regional and cultural preferences Advances in printing technology related to the Industrial Revolution enable newspapers to become an even more widely circulated means of communication. The Times acquired a printing press in 1814 capable of making 1,100 impressions per minute. Soon, it was adapted to print on both sides of a page at a time. This innovation made newspapers cheaper and thus available to a large part of the population. In 1830, the first penny press newspaper came into the market Lynde M. Walter's Boston Transcript. Penny press papers cot about one sixth price of the other newspapers and appealed to a wider audience. In France, Emile de Girardin started La Presse in 1836 introducing cheap advertising supported dailies to France. In 1848 August ang an Austrian who knew Girardin in Paris returned to Vienna to introduce the same methods with Die Presse.

Impact of Television and Internet

By the late 1990s the availability of news via television channels 24-hours and the internet posed an ongoing challenge to the business model of most newspapers in developed countries. Paid circulation has declined, while advertising revenue – which makes up the bulk of most newspapers income has been shifting from print media to new media, resulting in a general decline in profits. Many newspapers are around the launched online editions in an attempt to follow or stay ahead of their audience.

However, in the rest of the world, cheaper printing and distribution increased literacy, the growing middle class and other factors have more than compensated for the emergence of electronic media and newspapers continue to grow. On April 10, 1995 the American Reporter became the first daily newspaper, with its own paid reporters around the world and all-original content to start on the internet. The Editor-in-chief and founder is Joe Shea. The site is owned by 400 journalists.

Newspaper Categories

While most newspapers are aimed at a broad spectrum of readers, usually geographically defined some focus on groups of readers defined more by their interests than their location e.g., there are daily and weekly business newspapers and sports newspapers. Moreover specialist still are some weekly newspapers usually free and distributed within limited areas, these may serve communities as specific as certain settler populations or the local community.

Daily

A daily newspaper is issued every day, sometimes with the exception of Sundays and some national holidays. Saturday and Sunday editions of daily newspapers tend to be larger include more specialized sections and advertising inserts and cost more. Typically the majority of these newspapers staff work Monday to Friday so the Sunday and Monday editions largely depend on content done in advance or content that is syndicated. Most daily newspapers are published in the morning. Afternoon or evening papers are aimed more at commuters and office workers.

Weekly

The weekly newspapers are common and tend to be smaller than daily papers. In some cases, there are also newspapers that are published twice or three times a week. In the United States, such newspapers are generally still classified as weeklies.

National

Most of the nations have at least one newspaper that circulates throughout the country. A national newspaper was contrasted with a local newspaper serving a city or region. In the United Kingdom there are numerous national newspapers including the Independent, the Times, The Daily Telegraph, the Guardian, the Observer, the

Daily Mail, the Sun, the Daily Mirror and the Daily Express. In the United States and Canada, there are few national newspapers. Almost every market has one or two newspapers that dominate the area. Certain newspapers, notably The New York Times, the Wall Street Journal and USA Today in the US and the Globe and Mail and the National Post in Canada are available throughout the country. In India newspapers like the Times of India, the Hindu and the Hindustan Times are extremely popular and have large reader bases. Large metropolitan newspapers have also expanded distribution networks and with effort can be found outside their normal area.

International

There is also a small group of newspapers which may be characterized as International newspapers such as the International Herald Tribune have always had that focus, while others are repackaged national newspapers or international editions of national scale or large metropolitan newspapers. Often these international editions are scaled down to remove articles that might not interest the wider range of readers. As English became the international language of business and technology, many newspapers formerly published only in non-English languages have also developed English-language editions. In places as varied as Jerusalem and Mumbai newspapers are printed to a local and international English-speaking public. The advent of the internet has also allowed the non-English newspapers to put out a scaled down English version to give their newspaper a global outreach.

Online

Virtually all printed newspapers have online editions, which depending on the country may be regulated by journalism organizations such as the Press Complaints Commission in the UK. But as some publishers find their print-based models increasingly unsustainable, web-based newspapers have also started to appear such as the Southport Reporter in the UK and the Seattle Post-Intelligencer, which stopped publishing in print after 149 years in March 2009 and went online only.

Customized

A new trend in newspaper publishing is the introduction of individualization through on demand printing technology. Customized newspapers allow the reader to create their individual newspaper through the selection of individual pages from multiple publications. This 'best of' approach allows reviving the print-based model and opens up a new distribution channel to increase coverage beneath the usual boundaries of distribution.

Organization and personnel

In USA, the overall manager or chief executive of the newspaper is publisher in small newspapers, the owner of the publication is usually the publisher. Although he or she rarely or perhaps never writes stories, the publisher is legally responsible for the contents of the entire newspaper and also runs the business, including hiring editors, reporters and other staff members. This title is less common outside the US. The equivalent position in the film industry and television news shows is the executive producer.

Most newspapers have four main departments devoted to publishing the newspaper itself editorial, production/printing, circulation and advertising although they are frequently referred to by a variety of other names as well as non-newspaper specific departments also found in other businesses of comparable size, such as accounting, marketing, human resources and information technology. The English speaking world, the person who selects the content for the newspaper is usually referred to as the editor. Variations on this title such as editor-in-chief, executive editor and so on are common. For small newspapers, a single editor may be responsible for all content areas. At large newspapers, the most senior editor is overall in-charge of the publication, while next senior editors many focus on one subject area, such as local news or sports, these divisions are called news bureaus or desks and each is supervised by a designated editor.

Newspaper editors' copy edits the stories for their part of the newspaper, but they may share their workload with proofreaders and fact-checkers. Reporters are journalists, who primarily report facts that they have gathered. Reporters writing longer, less news-oriented articles may be called feature writers. Photographers and graphic artists provide images and illustrations to support articles. Journalists often specialize in a subject area called a beat, such as sport, religion or science. Columnists are journalists who write regular articles recounting their personal opinions and experiences.

Printers and press operators physically print the newspaper. Printing is outsourced by many newspapers, partly because of the cost of an offset web press and also a small newspapers' print run might be require less than an hour of operation, means if newspaper had its own press it would sit idle most of the time. If the newspaper offers information online, web masters and web designers may be employed to upload stories to the newspapers website. The staff of the circulation department communicates with retailers who sell the newspapers, subscriptions and supervise distribution of the printed newspapers through the mail by newspaper carriers, at retailers and through vending machines. Free newspapers do not sell subscriptions, but they still have a circulation department responsible for distributing the newspapers. Sales staff in the advertising department not only sells space to clients but also help advertisers design and plan their advertising campaigns. Other members of the advertising department may include graphic designers, who design ads according to the customers' specifications and the departments' policies. In an advertising free newspaper, there is no advertising department.

Zonal and other Editions

Newspapers often refine distribution of ads through zoning edition. Zoning occurs when advertising and editorial content change to replicate the location to which the product is delivered. The editorial content often may change merely to reflect alter in advertising – the quality and layout of which affects the space available for editorial or may contain region-specific news. In rare case, the advertising may not change from one zone to another, but there will be diverse region-specific editorial content. As the content can vary widely, zoned editions are often produced in parallel.

Editioning occurs in the main sections as news is updated throughout the night. The advertising is usually the same in each edition. Each edition represents the latest news available for the next press run, these editions are produced linearly, with one completed edition being copied and updated for the next edition. The previous edition is always copied to maintain a Newspaper of Record and to fall back on if a quick correction is needed for the press e.g., both the New York Times and Wall Street Journal offer a regional edition, printed through a local contractor and featuring local specific content. The journals' global advertising rate card provides a good example of editioning.

Newspaper circulation and readership

The number of copies distributed on an average day or on particular days is called the newspapers' circulation and is one of the principle factor used to set advertising rates. Circulation is not necessarily the same as copies sold, since some copies or newspapers are distributed without cost. Readership figure may be higher than circulation figures because many copies are read by more than one person, although this is offset by the number of copies distributed but not read.

According to the Guinness Book of World Records, the daily circulation of the Soviet newspaper 'Trud' exceeded 21,500,000 in 1990, while the Soviet weekly Argumenty I Fakty boasted the circulation of 33,500,000 in 1991. According to the United Nations information in 1995 Japan has three daily papers the Yomiuri Shimbun, Asahi Shimbun and Mainichi Shimbun with circulation was more than 5.5 million. Germany's Bild with a circulation of 3.8 million was the only other paper in that category. In the United Kingdom the Sun is the top seller, with around 3.24 copies distributed daily.

In India the Times of India is the largest circulation English newspaper with 3.14 million copies daily. According to 2009 Indian readership survey, the Dainik Jagran is the most read, local language (Hindi) newspaper with 55.70 million readers. In the US the Wall Street Journal has a circulation of approximately 2.01 million, making it the most widely distributed paper in the country. American newspaper was vending machine featuring news of the 1984 Summer Olympics.

A common measure of a newspaper's health is market penetration, expressed as a percentage of households that receive a copy of the newspaper against the total number of households in the paper's market area. In the 1920s on a national basis in the US daily newspapers achieved market penetration of 123 per cent. As other media began to compete with newspapers and printing became easier and less expensive giving rise to a greater diversity of publications, market penetration began to decline. It wasn't until the early 1970s. However the market penetration vaulted in below 100 per cent by 2000, it was 53 per cent.

Many paid-for newspapers offer a variety of subscription plans e.g, someone might want only a Sunday paper or perhaps only Sunday and Saturday may be only a work week subscription or perhaps a daily subscription. Most of the newspapers provide some or all of their content on the internet, either at no cost or for a fee. In some cases free access is available only for a matter of days or weeks after which readers must register and provide personal data. In other cases, free archives are provided.

Advertisement

Newspaper typically generates 70-80 per cent of its revenue from advertising and the remaining from sales and subscription. The major portion of the newspaper income is advertising is called editorial content, editorial matter or simply editorial, although the last term is also used to refer specifically to those articles in which the newspaper and its guest writers express their opinions. Newspapers have been hurt by the decline of many traditional advertisers. Department stores and supermarkets could be relied upon in the past to buy pages of newspaper advertisements, but due to industry consolidation are much less likely to do so now. Additionally, newspapers seeing traditional advertisers shift to new platforms. The classified category is shifting tc sites including craigslist, employment websites and auto sites.

National advertisers are shifting to many types of digital content including websites, rich media platforms and mobile. In recent years, the advertorial emerged. Advertorials are most commonly recognized as an opposite-editorial which third parties pay the fee. Advertorials commonly advertise new products or techniques such as a new design for golf equipment a new form of laser surgery or weight loss drugs. The tone is usually closer to that of a press release than of an objective news story.

Print vs. Online

Newspapers, since the dawn of internet have to contend with online media. These did not bring about the demise of printed newspapers. Reading newspaper print has a lower impact on global warming than reading online according to one of the world's leading papermakers. Reading a newspaper has a lower impact on global warming than reading the news online for 30 minutes. According to Torraspapel's paper the alternative to climate report change.

Role of Media in Modern Society

There are many different ways in which people communicate i.e., through phone, through personal encounters and by attending work place, school, seminars etc. Through media is not only communication medium used to dispense the flow of information, it also importance in developments of countries is worth mentioning as main source to inform people on political issues or current affairs as well as source of entertainment. The flow of information from one geographical location to another has increased in speed considerably with the advent in digitally enabled communication devices. Different network channels over cable or satellite TV, newspapers and radio channels are emerging at rapid pace providing the people with a medium to connect themselves with the outside world. Print media has always been a dominant medium throughout the decades in the western civilization, but it is the emergence of the television which has become the backbone of the global commercial development. Television contains the ability to produce multimedia content and thus has the immense power to change an individual's perception of reality. It is not a wonder that in order to believe in something, one has to have complete faith in the source of information. This source of information could be ranging from one person to any academic institution. However in today's connected society it is the media, which has become the main source of information. The role of media is playing a main source of information is a controversial issue. It is being debated what are the media functions in a society and what are its impact on individual. The term media is a general term is not restrict to a particular entity but in order to understand the term commercial media, the US provides the best platform for critically analyzing the role of media in a society. Regardless of what type of sources of media are analyzed from newspapers to network channels.

Media and our Society

Throughout the year it has been a proven fact that media has a lasting effect on our society. The rising question through, is how is this media affecting our society? It is affecting us in good ways, bad ways or both? There's no question that media has changed over the years and there more media now then ever before. The biggest hope of all is how people think media influences and changes what a person does or thinks. The people who say this may be right, but in certain extent. With that I have found the three major sources of media today are: the news, advertising and music.

For most American families used to be normal to go home and turn on the news to find out what's going on out there in the big world, but lately that doesn't seem to be the case. If I asked you to name fifteen positive things that you can remember seeing on the news this past six months, do you think could? My best bet would be no. The news stations know what draws people's attention in most, and in human nature, that's negativity. Sure, there are positive things that are shown too, but very few. Society has found that the news is no longer enjoyable to watch and find they turning the channel before done. Why is this though? Is the news becoming too much for people to handle? In complaint, some would even go as far as saying that events portrayed on the news leads to more of those same crimes being repeated later on. Is this all in theory, or the truth? Many studies over the past few decades have reported that viewing this violence encourages aggressive behaviour and teaches violent resolution to conflicts. Although I think that the point of news was supposed to be just the opposite. In this day and age, what the news may not fully understand is that it sells what it sells what it shows. But if you look back to when television news was first aired you will realize that it was started to inform the world, not sell.

Social Responsibility of the Press Media

1. *Educate the public:* People can explore at firsthand but a tiny fraction of the world of which he is a part. To know and understand the world, man must depend largely on the printed word. Not only can the press furnish man with the information he needs to formulate his own ideas but it can also stimulate him by offering him the ideas of others. For centuries, the press has been regarded as an important carrier of information and ideas. Running through John Milton's Areopagitica of 1644 is the the them that a free press is indispensable in the quest for truth. As Milton put it, where there is much desire to learn, there of necessity will be much arguing much writing, many opinions, for opinion in good men is but knowledge in the making. Although Thomas Jefferson wrote no unified work on the press, his scatttered wrings time and again touch upon the importance of a free press to public enlightenment. In a letter to M. Coray in 1823, he remarked: 'the Press is the best instrument for enlightening the mind of man and improving him as a rational, normal and social being.
2. *Help to the political system:* Closely allied with the public enlightenment function of the press is the second function of servicing the political system. The nature of democratic government imposes a heavy responsibility on the press, which is granted a privileged position under the constitution. As Carl Becker once remarked, 'Democratic government rests on the assumption that the people are capable of governing themselves better than any one or a few can do it for them. If the citizens are to rule themselves wisely, they must be aware of the issues and problems at stake and must have access to views and

information on which to base sound decisions. Therefore, the press must serve as an engine of democracy, as a transmission belt between the people and their elected representatives. The very success of government may depend in large measure on the extent to which the press services the political system and the extent to which the people make wise use of the press.

3. *Profitable manner*: The traditional concept of media is freedom provide cogent justification to a fourth function of the press – making profitable manner through proper use of its freedom. The theory holds that that only a free press operating under a system of private enterprise, can fulfil the tasks of enlightening the public servicing the political system and safeguarding personal liberties. The syllogism behind that assumption runs somewhat as follows: only a free press can serve the cause of truth. A press beholden to the government or to any special interest group cannot be free, because it will inevitably be subjected to environmental and financial pressures. Therefore, to be free to present news and views without fear of favour, the press must be a self sufficient business enterprise. Carried a step further, this line of reasoning has been used to justify large communications enterprises. The argument is that a large prosperous medium is better able to withstand pressures than a small, marginal one. The entry of the government into the communications field, according to traditional theory, is bad. For one thing, governmental media would no doubt be more interesting in perpetuating the party in power than in truth. For another thing, a subsidised governmental press would threaten the economic sufficiency of a private enterprise press. With no need to show a profit, such a press would have an unfair economic advantage over the regular commercial press.

4. *Assist the economic system*: Related to the profit-making function is a fifth task of the press, one which emerged with the development of modern advertising, that of servicing the economic system. Long before advertising assumed the importance it has today, the press fulfilled this task to some extent. In Colonial America, newpapers filled their columns

with information about commerce and shipping, material important to an economy in which foreign trade and commerce continued to flourish, even after the penny press of the 1830s made its pitch for the masses with human-interest copy. But it was the rise of a compiled system of mass production and mass distribution that the contribution of the press to the national economy became of major importance. Today a task of the press is to bring together through advertising, the buyers and sellers of goods and services. In performing that seemingly simple task, the press according to some scholars has helped to promote a dynamic, expanding economy.

5. *Providing entertainment*: almost from the time that Caxton introduced printing to England, the press has devoted a part of its output to entertainment. However moralizing may have been their tone, the broadside ballads which flourished in Britain for more than three centuries,were intended less for edification than for amusement. Other offerings pamphlets and books were also intended to amuse the reader. Early newspapers in England and America were primarily informational, but they too can human-interest copy from time to time. As the press tapped mass audiences, there seems to have been an increase in the proportion of material frankly designed to afford amusement, entertainment or escape. Today, serving up entertainment seems to be one of the main functions of the press.

6. *Evaluating the services of the press*: Historicaly, some of them are of longer standing than others. Public enlightenment is one of the oldest functions, servicing the economic system is a relatively recent addition. As has been shown, some of the functions are inherent in the theory of political freedom. The responsibilities of the press for enlightening the public, for servicing the political system and for safeguarding personal liberties are intimately identified with the Anglo-American concept of freedom of the pree. At least one of the functions, however, is not inherent in the theory. The role of the press in servicing the economic system was recognised only after the development of modern advertising.

7. *Problem involved in publishing*: What hinders the press in carrying out its functions? There are many things. There are limitations imposed by the communication process itself – by way in which we send and receive spoken and written messages. There are limitations imposed by the nature of the media. But two major problems concentration of ownership of the media and the commercial basis of the press system.

8. *Concentration of ownership of the press*: The concentration of ownership of the press which has resulted from among other things, technological advances and the demands by readers for improved service has alarmed many observes. In the daily newspapers field, the number of papers has gone steadily downward as circulations have steadily mounted. As the number of dailies has diminished, more and more cities have been left without competing newspapers. Nixon has throughly documented this situation.

9

Role of Internet

Despite the negative effects of the internet, intelligent use of it provides a verity of information relating to business, education, examination results, employment, matrimonial, research etc. It is particularly very much useful for students, teachers and researchers as an economic way of collecting desired information in course of preparing reports and conducting researches. Again it provides facilities for e-mailing. The youth should therefore, take the advantage of positive use of this modern medium. It is pertinent here to state that while recommending to build a knowledge network interconnecting our knowledge institutions and infrastructure with access speeds of 100Mbps and more with a view to give a major push to collaborations and sharing needed to enhance the quality of our education, research and applications and at the same time to empower our people to be competitive in global economy the National Knowledge Commission (2007) rightly stressed the utility of internet in this knowledge era.

The internet has provided an ideal solution by presenting many articles in multiple languages and permitting the viewer to select the language of his choice. It also elimination of printing and postage costs makes publishing such electronic journals far more economically practical. Another advantage of the internet is the simplicity of making corrections, additions and updates to an article when necessary, a virtual impossibility with conventional printed journals. In addition, with such increased international cooperation, a multi disciplinary panel of experts could eventually be established to serve as a peer review broad for future papers submitted for publication.

The internet is a massive network of computers from around the world all connected by cable and satellite. When users are connected to the internet they can receive text, images, video and sound on their computer from computers anywhere in the world. Just as there is a book or magazine on nearly every subject in local libraries, bookshops or newsagents, so is there information on virtually every subject on the internet. The internet is also called the world wide wed. With the use of internet, it is possible to receive/ transmit information containing images, graphics sound and videos. ISP industry can offer services as:

- Linking consumers and businesses via internet.
- Monitoring/maintaining customer's web sites.
- Network management/systems integration.
- Backbone access services for other ISP's.
- Managing online purchase and payment systems.

The internet is designed to be indefinitely extendible and the reliability of internet primarily depends on the quality of the service providers' equipments. The limitation of the internet is security and privacy and threats are hackers, viruses etc whereas the benefits of internet are:

- Doing fast business.
- Trying out new ideas.
- Gathering opinions.
- Allowing the business to appear alongside other established businesses.
- Improving the standards of customer service/support resource.
- Supporting managerial functions.

There are several characteristics of the internet that may be seen to increase its potential for harmful to children. These would includes: the easy access for users, abundance of material available, its ubiquity and affordability, interactivity of the medium and the potential for individual users to share material, degree of anonymity that users can enjoy and the lack of gate-keepers or authorities that might restrict access. However, these are also the characteristics that are often seen as crucial to the benefits of the medium in terms of facilitating learning, communication, civic participation etc.

Several of the concern that arise in relation to the internet have been carried over from older media and strength be seen to affect in other everyday contexts, although the internet does provide framework in which people may say and do things that they would not face-to-face.

We need to be wary of overstatement it is clear there are some new dangers here for children as well as indeed for adults also. In particular, while giving out personal information is necessary for a whole range of commercial and non-commercial transactions. It also places the individual at risk in generally unprecedented ways. There is a growing body of research on children's and young people use of the internet. Here again, it is potential to identify different research ethnicity, although the situation is by no means as polarized as it is in the case of games. Mainstream communications research has generally avoided the experimental approaches employed in relation to games, tending instead to use large-scale questionnaire surveys to map patterns in access and use.

Given the rapid change of technological and cultural change such studies often have a fairly limited self-life and need to be frequently updated. Further, a great deal of this work is essentially expressive e.g., when it comes to potentially harmful or offensive material, we do know a fair amount at least from self-report data-about whether children is likely to have encountered such material and in very broad terms how they feel about it. However, we know relatively little from this research about how they interpret this material and almost nothing about its effects. Differently, researchers in media and cultural studies have tended to rely on smaller-scale qualitative research. The focus here has been on how families or specific groups of children interact online and make sense of what they encounter. The questions here focus on issues such as identity construction, peer culture and play and on the social or domestic contexts in which the internet is used. While these issues might be considered in terms of effects: is peer group online interaction more positive than offline? How does the internet affect the quality of family life?

The researchers tend to avoid addressing such issues in this way. Again, the emphasis is on taking a holistic view rather than thinking in terms of cause and effect, it is argued that we need to situate children's uses of the internet within a broader social and cultural context in which multiple factors are in play. This approach tends to emphasize children's agency and autonomy and at the same time can come close to celebratory account. Even the two approaches have identified and there is no means of mutually exclusive and some of the best research in the field manages to combine them.

Over the past three years, in cooperation with the collegamento pro-Sindone a number of articles previously available only in one language have been translated into multiple languages and reprinted on the respective websites. In addition, though the efforts of the Cento Espanola do Sindonologia, a Spanish language website has been online for over a year. Non-received articles have also been reprinted for the benefit of researchers and the lay public alike. The Scientific papers and Articles page of the website already includes many of these. One of the greatest challengers to modern shroud research is finding and accessing previously published work. Even with access to a sophisticated research library, many references are very hard to find. Through the cooperation of all of the world's largest shroud collections, a massive bibliography of books and articles has been compiled and is found on the Shroud Booklist page of the shroud of Turin website and the scientific articles page of the collegamento pro-Sindone website. Finally, easily accessible centrally locted bibliographies are available to everyone.

Along these lines, even when a reference is determined, it is often impossible to find the actual paper or journal, many important references are out of print and more than twenty years old. Over the last three years, rights have been obtained to reprint a number of these on the website and more are being added constantly. This will be continued and in time, the network of shroud websites will become the central repositories and primary resources of shroud data for sindonologists worldwide. These often take the form of responses to articles and personal correspondence between individual researchers. The website has already been host to a number of such debates though the good graces of all the participants who have made their materials available for publication. This feature will be expanded and grow to provide a true open international forum for continued discussion that allows other interested parties to enter the debate.

Conferences such as this one have also benefited from using the internet. I regularly checked the Richmond Center website for the up-to-date schedule of the speakers planned for this event and to see the amount of available seating that remained and of course, the final papers presented here will eventually be published on the internet to supplement the production of a written acts or printed proceedings. Already in place on the shroud of Turin website is the 'research registry page' where many researchers have already advertised for material they needed. These have included blood and linen samples, rare books or articles and access to special facilities. In some cases, organizations or individuals with resources to offer for shroud research have posted them on the site to make them available to those who might need them.

With the continued worldwide interest in the shroud, many researchers are often called upon by lay and professional groups to make presentations and give lectures. An international shroud Speakers Directory has recently been added to the website. This provides organizations looking for such speakers a central source of qualified experts to select from. Listings include biographies, topics and geographic availability of each speaker. Another useful function of the website is the gathering of statistical information and data. Some researchers have designed a questionnaire that website viewers fill out and send in. The researchers will receive the information via e-mail and can integrate the responses directly into their analysis.

The increased use of the internet for research by students and scientists necessitated the development of a standardized notation for citing references taken from the web. This has been researched and a number of suggested formats are now included on key pages of the website. Also the growth in other, specialized shroud websites, particularly those geared towards students has provided added resources for the next generation of shroud researchers. The efficient manner of reprinting technical scientific papers was needed that kept the resident symbols, scientific notation, graphs, charts, illustrations and photographs intact over the last three years. New technologies for viewing images on the internet are rapidly becoming available and several are destined to become standards. These are being carefully tracked to determine their future value for website viewers. One such format, live picture, allows viewers to zoom in and out or pan across large, high resolution images using a plug-in to their internet browser software. We hope to add this powerful feature soon and allow viewers to examine the subtlest details of the shroud of Turin at their leisure. Finally, a search capability will be added in the near future that will allow website viewers to enter key words and quickly search through the entire website to find information specific to their needs. This will be particularly useful as the quantity of materials on the site increases.

Recent developments in communication technology have provided us with powerful new tools for instant global communications. With the advent of these new technologies, the obstacles to creating an international shroud center have been eliminated and the center is already open for business. But in this case, the center resides in cyberspace rather than in a physical location and instead of a single website, the center is actually a growing network of shroud related websites around the world, linked together and cooperating to create an exciting and fertile environment for sharing shroud information and presenting ideas from every point of view. The role of the internet in shroud research is no longer a thing of the future. It is today's reality.

Unwanted contact

It leads to a further are of risk, which is that of unwanted contract. The main focus of concern here is on so-called stranger danger i.e., the possibility of threatening contract from unknown adults, particularly pedophiles. Such apprehension about the internet needs to be situated in the broader context of growing apprehension about risks to children offline. Parents' fears of the likelihood of their children being abducted and abused by unknown strangers have risen significantly in recent years, perhaps partly swollen by the high-profile reporting of rare but nevertheless disturbing cases. While the actual incidence of attacks and abductions has not significantly increased, parents are now much more keen to confine their children to the home and to provide them with media and technology that will make the child's bedroom a more smart alternative to the evident dangers of the outside world. Paradoxically in doing they have created the possibility that stranger danger will now be imported into the obvious safety of the family home.

The past study reports that many children have contract online with people whom they do not know, although there has been little research looking in any details at the nature of such contact or at how children respond. Of course, it is possibility of such online contract may be a very positive thing, e.g., it allows children to discuss concerns that cannot be shared with people offline or if it brings them into contract with others from very different cultural backgrounds. In certain cases, online contracts lead to face-to-face meetings, although most of this contract is with people of a similar age and it would be quite wrong to imply that much of it is any more dangerous than contracts that young people might make in any other setting. Of course, it would be negative to deny that the internet has provided pedophiles with new opportunities for contract with children and these risks may have increased with the advent of mobile platforms.

The present all Medias, changes in technology go hand to hand with changes in social use. Only a few years ago, anxiety about online encounters with strangers focused on children's use of chartrooms. Recent research suggested that chartroom use is declining, while use of instant messaging is widespread and suggesting that children prefer to communicate with friends rather than strangers. At the same time, new opportunities to meet strangers online have appeared, such as via online games, though these encounters are less likely to lead to actual meetings and more likely to be confined to the context of play in a fictional world.

Some researchers suggested that the teaching through online is risky. That means the children's are less likely to become victims. However, other researchers suggested that the majority of children are already very well aware of potential risks here and yet this does not tend to prevent them from making such contracts. This would suggest that some young people may actively seek out risk in this context e.g., various forms of flirting and this may be particularly the case for children who are less satisfied with their offline lives. At the same time, there is also a danger that the figure of the predatory pedophile has become a kind of contemporary bogeyman and such warnings are somehow seen as irrelevant to children's own lives. As this implies, there is a need for education about such risks that goes well beyond one dimensional warning of the just say no variety and as we shall see in the following section notions of risk and privacy are becoming increasingly complex in the online environment.

Another different kind of unwanted contract is that of bullying. Again, there is evidence that a significant number of children have experienced online bullying. The internet clearly permits bullying to occur more secretly and yet to be distributed more widely e.g., through the copying and forwarding of images. However, the fact remains that many more children are bullied offline than online and there is no evidence that the internet has led to an increase in bullying to distressing it may be. How online bullying might support offline bullying and the new combinations of techniques that might emerge remain an issue for further research.

Online Violence

There is a little doubt that the internet has made it significantly easier to distribute material that provokes violence of various kinds. Such material would comprise hate sites as well as material that appear to support or celebrate forms of self-harm. Surveys suggest that a significant minority of children have been seen such material and while they generally few of them is dislike. Particularly it can find disturbing. There is again relatively detailed evidence about how children interpret such material and even less about its potential effects. In case of hate sites, much of the research has tended to focus on the analysis of content. Violence among individuals might not otherwise be disposed to accept it. Some have argued that such sites may be relatively ineffective as recruitment tools among adults.

The other studies suggested that depends on the directness and narrative content of the messages. One French study suggested that such material may have the reverse effect of encouraging critical attitudes towards racism among young people. The legal implications of this situation are complex and some of the sites could be prosecuted in the UK under laws on incitement to ethnic hatred, although in the first amendment is likely to offer protection. Meanwhile, there are several educational projects that attempt to children to biases and distortions in such material.

A related phenomenon is that extreme self-help sites related to topics such as eating disorders and suicide. Sites that positively celebrate forms of self-harm or provide advice on how to carry it out more effectively are certainly disturbing and in the past has been deleted or blocked by service providers. Some research suggests that such sites may normalize self harming behaviour. Others have argued that they can support the useful offer that might not be elsewhere and giving voice to such issues is preferable to silencing them. Again the question is raised by such sites, whether they result in an increase in harmful behaviour or simply shift it in a different direction and this is a question on which there is no definitive evidence.

The benefits of the Internet

The potential risks of the internet needs to be balanced against an understanding of its potential benefits. The positive effects of the internet is claims to tent to focus on the value of instant access to information and its role in creating new forms of communication and community. This can be seen particular consequences e.g., in building or renewing civic participation in generating tolerance and global understanding in providing new opportunities for creative expression and overcome social isolation. Popular accounts make much of the new skills and knowledge that are being developed by the so-called digital generation and of the liberating potential of the medium for young people. Such accounts tend to present the internet as an enormous power for social wellbeing. It is seen to offer great possibilities for self-expression, creativity and learning and to bring about great openness, tolerance and trust.

Academic commentary has frequently sought to puncture some of the inflated claims that are made about the benefits of the internet and the forms of technological determinism that tend to characterize them. Ultimately, while the technologically empowered cyber kids of the popular imagination may indeed exist, they are certainly in a minority and are untypical of young people as a whole. Researchers suggested that the majority of young people are not interested in technology in its own right, but simply in what they can do with it. There is relatively little evidence of young people using the internet to develop global connections. In most of the cases it appears to be used primarily as a means of reinforcing local networks among peers. Warschauer pointed out that the potential for multimedia production which requires the latest computers and software and high bandwidth is actually quite inaccessible to all but the wealthy middle classes. Researchers also suggests that young people may be less fluent or technologically literate in their use of the internet than is often assumed. Observational studies suggest that the young people often encounter considerable difficulties in using search engines.

Regarding to the games, the benefit of the internet for young people are predominantly framed in terms of education. It is evidence of the educational value of the internet is somewhere ambiguous. Arguments about the value of instant access to a wealth of information are typically countered with evidence about the proliferation of plagiarism and cut and paste approaches to academic work. The evidence is that technology in itself will serve as a means of raising educational achievements in schools or indeed that it is worthy of the money that is spent on it is far persuasive. As in the case of games, it is clear that the educational benefits of the internet are not automatic or guaranteed rather then they derive from the ways in which it is used. In relation to schools, the educational value of the medium depends very much on the classroom strategies that teachers employ, while in the home, the role of parental support is crucial. As this implies, the benefits of the medium do not follow automatically from simply gaining access rather than they depend very much on the skills and competencies that are developed by users.

Despite these necessary qualifications, it would be quite wrong to underestimate the significance benefits that the internet can offer young people, in terms of learning, communication, creativity and social relationships. The accessibility of global reach is simplicity and flexibility of the medium and indeed the vast extent of material that it brings together does offer significant opportunities for support in learning, for pursuing entertainment and leisure interests an for creating new democratic forms of communication and cultural expression. While something to remain outside the digital world, those who do access to it tend to regard. It is an enormously positive phenomenon and indeed as a necessity of modern life and they feel that the children who do not use it are at a significant disadvantage in respect of educationally, socially and culturally. While this is predictably less of an issue for younger children by the time they reach the teenage years. The internet comes to equal television and mobile phones as a must have medium for young people.

Research to Policy Creation

There is certain proof of specific kinds of harm and offence that can arise from young people's use of the internet. While the evidence on the harm resulting from mainstream pornography is fairly limited, there is no doubt that many other phenomena considered here can be considered directly harmful or at least offensive. Whether they are more harmful than equivalent phenomena offline e.g., whether online bullying is more dangerous than offline bullying could be a matter for debate. At the same time, there is a great claim about the benefits of the internet. In respect of internet, the educational value of children and young people. Many of these claims are inflated and in several cases the evidence from research is some extent limited. Nevertheless, it would be foolish to deny that the internet has considerable potential to benefit children, even if the realization of that potential depends very much on the circumstances in which the medium is used.

The obvious difficulty that arises when seeking to apply research to policy is that of balancing the potential risks and benefits, while recognizing that both are frequently overstated. Fatherly, particular forms of regulation may be considered desirable; these also raise significant legal and technical issues. In respect of the former, the arguments for free speech cannot be ignored and it could be argued that they need to be considered particularly carefully when one is addressing the activities of minority or fringe groups of any kind. On the other hand some types of material considered here are clearly illegal and covered by existing laws. In respect of technology, the evidence suggests that attempts to filter or block access to particular types of internet content, whether in home or public settings such as schools, have rarely proven effective. As Frechette suggests, the software industry is currently generating significant profits from parental anxieties about inappropriate content. Although such software often defines what is inappropriate in narrow ways.

Evidence suggests that the effectiveness of such devices e.g., in schools is decidedly limited. Filters are typically very crude and unreliable and young people complain about how they block access to sites that are needed for perfectly legitimate educational reasons. Researcher also suggest that the use of filters is frequently resisted. School students will often claim that they can evade filters, through a range of inventive and devious strategies and some even boast of their skill in hacking into teaching staff files. The limitation of filtering or blocking programs appears to be accepted even by researchers who strongly agree with them in principle. There is also a danger that too prohibitive or protective an attitude in schools may lead to young people simply giving up on internet use in schools and reverting to home use. This has particular implications for young people whose access at home is limited and it also means that productive educational use – as well as education about risk become much more difficult.

The implication of such findings is that a more educational

strategy is required. There have been some significant educational interventions focused on internet risk and on related issues such as hate sites. In some cases, such strategies have proven less than effective not least because they tend to be narrowly defined and fail to connect with young people's perceptions of issues such as risk and privacy. However, research does suggest that parental intervention and involvement can enhance children's ability to understand web content, to handle risk and use the medium effectively and there is also evidence of successful programmes being developed in schools. However, it should be emphasized that digital literacy is not simply a matter of being able to use technological tools, but also of critically understanding information. The implications of such an approach will be discussed in more detail in the final section of this report.

New and Emerging Media

The median landscape is rapidly changes and as new media forms emerge, so that new concerns about their possible effects. This section focuses on a range of relatively new phenomena, including social networking sites, user-generated content, online communities and social worlds, online gaming and peer to peer file sharing. The academic research on these developments is still in its infancy and so this discussion draws on more speculative and non-academic accounts, some of which have yet to be published. These phenomena continue to evoke well-established concerns of the kind considered above, albeit sometimes in new forms. Social networking sites e.g., generated new anxieties about stranger danger and bullying while file-sharing and user generated content sites have provided new opportunities for circulating sexually explicit or violent material that some consider inappropriate for children. Familiar concerns about addiction about the demise of healthy family life or about the physical effects of excessive use, have all been expressed once more in respect of these new phenomena.

Equally, enthusiasts for Web 2.0 have proclaimed its potential for promoting creative self-expression, interactive communication and democratic participation in the media. These positive and negative consequences must ultimately be seen as two sides of the same coin. These new phenomena do raise new concerns or lend some hitherto fairly marginal concerns a new intensity. Before taking each of these phenomena in turn, it is worth identifying four broader issues that cut across these different areas, particularly relating to the question of risk:

1. **Privacy:** New media forms a social networking sites and blogs posses a form of intimacy. They are easily accessible in the public domain. Users may reveal highly personal information in the belief that they are doing for an audience consisting only of their friends. They may forget, or fail to fully register, the fact that this information is visible to others and indeed to parents, teachers or employers as much as potentially dangerous strangers. This situation provides important new opportunities for sexual predators and for bullying by peers as well as for various forms of deception and identity theft. However, it also raises more far-reaching questions about the changing ways in which young people understand the boundaries between the public and the private issue that has also emerged in relation to phenomena such as reality television and the continuing rise of celebrity culture.
2. **Trust and Credibility:** The new occurrences emphasize existing concerns about how users evaluate online information e.g., Wikipedia is an online user-generated encyclopedia that is very widely cited by students as an authoritative source, although there have been significant critics of the quality of its content. Meanwhile, the rise of blogging has further facilitated the rapid circulation of hate speech, deceptive rumours and conspiracy theories of all kinds. New media offer the benefit of a much wider range of information, but the motivations, identity and quality of those sources are often difficult to ascertain. Communities of users may develop their own standards for judging and maintaining credibility, although this process can be fraught with disputes but very often it is down to individual users to decide what and whom they should trust. In this respect, the media pose significant educational challenges: 'wiring up' schools or homes and assuming that

the social good of information will flow through the screen is at best naïve and at worst positively dangerous.

3. **Commercialism:** Web 2.0 appears to be area in which ordinary users rather than large commercial companies are the authors and owners of content. However, key Web 2.0 site are owned by large global media corporations and offer extensive opportunities for high targeted advertising which is why they are changing hands for billions of dollars. Auxiliary, users of such sites are often required to provide significant amounts of personal information, which can be used by companies as a basis for further promotional activities, is called as 'data-mining'. In other situations, commercial messages may be deeply embedded in the form of branding or promotions in content that outwardly appears to be a harmless form of play. Unlike television or print advertising the commercial dimensions of these activities may be effectively invisible to children and in deed to adults.
4. **Intellectual Property:** The potential of digital technology in terms of copying and circulating content has significantly implications for the notion of copyright and intellectual property. This is most evident case with file-sharing, where copyright material is exchanged illegally by users, and in the rising incidence of academic plagiarism. However, it also applies to the way in which content can be quoted or 'cut and pasted' into very different contexts from that in which it was originally presented. As the intellectual ownership of content is undermined, there is a danger that any ethical responsibility for the consequences of one's communicative actions tends to be dissipated. In this respect, a situation does not only affect the profits of large corporations, but also the communication rights of individuals.

All these dimensions could be seen at present risks for young people. To a large extent, these are risks of the routine rather than the spectacular variety, although in some respects they may be more acute because they are relatively subtle, and because they are not necessarily recognized by teachers, parents or caregivers. Here again, these risks can be seen as an inevitable corollary of the apparent freedom and flexibility that is afforded by new media. In this sense, the issue then becomes not so much one of preventing or neutralizing these risks, but of enabling young people to deal with them on their own behalf. In the following pages, we consider the implications of these issues in relation to a series of specific areas.

Social Networking Services

Social networking sites i.e., MySpace, Facebook and Bebo are some of the most popular online destinations for young people today. These sites provides home pages on which the user can display their personal profile including information such as location, interests and tastes as well as photos or videos, music tracks and links to friends pages. Home page may also include facilities for chat; file sharing, blogging and discussion groups. These sites have many attractions and benefits for young people. These include being able to meet people with the same interests and find like-minded communities the ability to discuss sensitive issues anonymously in potentially supportive environment and the opportunities for self-expression which are not possible to the same degree in face-to-face situations. These benefits shoot partly from the anonymity and the global reach afforded by the internet. Anonymity is most obviously important in discussions concerning sensitive issues. Such situations can also overcome the disadvantages of some face-to-face environment in which there are unequal power relationships. The potential reach of social networks has been important to young artists as a way of developing an audience for their productions and this also aids young people who might otherwise be limited to face-to-face interactions in smaller communities or in communities in which they have minority interest.

Many of the general concerns connected with children and young people use the internet discussed in emerge in social networking. Anonymity brings risks as well as benefits particularly around contract. There is concern that online social networking is bringing bullying into the home outside of school hours, a different experience from face-to-face bullying which is more limited in terms of time and place. Some researchers suggested that girls may be risk of being bullied in this way. Issues of trust are connected to bullying when trust is established on a false basis and then intentionally broken in order to cause emotional harm. Trust and anonymity are also key issues in relation to grooming practices in which older men portray themselves as younger for the purpose of seducing under age girls. The extent to which sexual abuse is occurring through social networking services is questionable. However, it is still the case that the vast majority of sexual abuse occurs in the home and between known contacts where the adult is clearly recognizable. The other concern is relevant here about greater access to hate speech or other anti-social content. In this concern the young people are finding support for activities that the young people are finding support for activities that they otherwise would not found. However, it is unclear about the behaviour and attitudes change when in contact with social networks or people are simply sharing ideas with a wider community than previously available to them.

There are more subtle issues that relate to social network to do with privacy and trust and these are also tied in with the commercial component of social networking services. As evidenced by the recent high-profile sales of social networking sites, this is a highly commodities enterprise. E-market research estimates that revenue from social networking advertisements will amount of $1.9 billion in total by 2011 and marketers are seeing these advertisements as a key point of access to the pocket books of young people. Online marketing on social network site includes data mining information on users' pages and then 'hypo-targeting' individual users with personalized advertisements based on demographic and psychographic data. New social advertising programs are capable of collating individual users actions across a variety of websites and can also access to individuals list of friends for advertising purposes. In addition to these developments, various companies have established their own pages on social networking sites in attempting to capture a young audience these pages frequently offer incentives for users to engage with them or become a friend or fan.

Finally conversational advertising aims at providing young people with branded materials which they use, share and discuss with friends.

The young people are well aware of the risk of sharing personal information, they see in social networking sites as private or peer defined spaces. Research shows that online social networking is seen as part of youth culture, the point of having a page is to be part of peer network, to define one's identity for a wider social group to negotiate and manage public identity and to build a community of friends. Young people see social networking sites as spaces for play, often submitting false information or jointly constructing a single page with a group of friends. Perhaps because social networking is an important part of many youth cultures and traditionally youth cultures centre on practices that are separate from younger children and from adults, it is possible that young people do not see these online practices as public.

Although social networking pages can be marked as private by the user, policies vary from site to site: some services withhold information marked private from marketers, while others, like Facebook, sell such information for marketing purposes, even after a user has quit a service. The research is showing that the companies' privacy policies are difficult to understand and young people are in need of training in order to make the most of the facilities available to them on social networking sites. They are used at present, the private/public settings do not completely meet the needs of young people socializing online.

The privacy options are geared toward individual interactions which do not provide users with the flexibility they need to handle conflicts within groups of friends. Recent reports suggested that the information about young people post online is sometimes used when they apply for jobs, internships, clubs or schools as well as by organizations. There is a need here to develop young people's critical understanding of the public nature of social networking sites as well as the privacy setting available to them. Although media literacy will help in this regard, the companies themselves can also take action.

User Generated Content

Beyond the more customized facilities offered by social networking sites, there is a range of other participatory sites such as wikis, blogs and image-sharing sites, which are designed specifically for users to upload, share or view content. Also there are more personal forms of user-generated content such as e-mail and instant messaging, which are also discussed here. Many social networking sites involve creating content and vice-versa, sites that are focused on user-generated content have the capacity to build social networks and there are clear connections between this section and the previous one. As with social networking sites, young people's desire to interact with media in social, personal and expressive ways is driving the popularity of user-generated content sites. There may even be some unsetting of traditional relationships between media producers and consumers here. We know of at least one school age student who is a senior editor with Wikipedia – an experience of participation in knowledge creation unthinkable in the era of the print encyclopedia.

It is clear that young people are viewing and contributing to sites which include user-generated content, with a study in 2007 indicating that as many as 57 per cent of online teenagers post their own content to such sites. Sharing and discussing media on user-generated content sites such as YouTube is one way in which young people are socializing, much in the same way other media are used in social relationships. User-generated content sites are also seen to be offering young people spaces in which they can have a voice. The opportunity to create and distribute one's own media is being hailed by some as providing the means to a more democratic media environment.

The ease of sharing media and the global reach of such network is leading to the emergence of new participatory cultures online, which may have particular benefits for young people. Jenkins et.al. assert that these participatory cultures build on traditional skills, but the specific new media literacy are also developing. Rather than being based simply on technological skills, this new media literacy involves a set of cultural competencies and social skills. He also identifies eleven new skills associated with online social environments, including appropriation, multitasking, collective intelligence, judgment, networking and negotiation. Importantly, however, educators also have a role to play here. He also outlines three concerns in relation to participatory media cultures which point to a need for educational intervention: the participation gap, the transparency problem and the ethics challenge. In relation to user-generated content, the ethics challenge and the transparency problem are key risks which are discussed in this section.

The ethics challenge discussed by Jenkins et al. includes questions about representation i.e., how young people are presenting themselves, their peers and other materials for comment e.g., in blogs or through photos and videos. There are also questions here about how young people understand the immediate or long-term impacts of such representations on other individuals or social groups. On a wider level, there are ethical questions concerning intellectual property and copyright. The creative commons movement recognizes the benefit of allowing people to share and build on each other's ideas and work. However, it is not uncommon on user-generated sites for young people to draw or build on copyrighted material that does not operate under a creative commons license. Large companies are increasingly tracking the use of their content in spaces such as personal WebPages, social networking sites or YouTube in seeking to identify and prosecute people for copyright infringements. Recently, the Entertainment Software Association called for the implementation of a piracy curriculum for children aged 5 to 11.

Young people's involvement in participatory culture offers a range of benefits in terms of learning, users are making judgments about content, building collective knowledge for the purpose of assessment, comparing and critiquing representations. All of which are helping to develop their skills in critical evaluation. However, assessing the credibility online content remains a key concern, in relation both to information and to social interaction. Engaging in online communication entails making judgments about whether e-mails or instant messages are from people who can be trusted, about whether comments expressed on a blog or in response to user-generated content are valid, authority and expertise of the participants.

Commercial interest also impinge on the credibility of user-generated content, with special e-mail techniques being used by companies which capitalize on friendship networks, promotional blogs set up by companies which appear to be written by an individual with no commercial interest or connection and content posted on chat sites, forums, image sharing sites or informational web pages for the purpose of promotion. As outlined above, online environments are seen as an important means of capturing the increasingly lucrative youth market. In terms of user-generated content, companies are supplying young people with more ways to interact with their brands, including branded instant messaging sites, contests for contributing video or music to advertisements and branded content for instant messaging, blogging or other personal webpage. Whether young people understand, resist, ignore or manipulate these commercial messages is an area for further research.

Online Communities and Online Worlds

The idea of the online or virtual community is by now well established, and there is a significant body of literature relating to this phenomenon. Studies of text based online communities such as forums, chartrooms and bulletin boards, where participants meet to discuss common interests, have explored both the positive and negative aspects of life within such settings. A number of concerns relating to teenage users of such sites overlap with those that have arisen around social networking. A key area of interest has been the ways in which online communities may support dangerous, harmful or illegal activities. Aside from concerns relating to contract with paedophiles, other dangers have also been identified. Recent discussion of suicide pacts between internet users who meet online has suggested that depressed adolescents may be vulnerable. The suggestion through internet chartrooms and websites encourage anorexia and bulimia amongst teens has also been expressed. Although other researchers have challenged this idea, the internet services company Yahoo has appeared to endorse this position by taking down pro-anorexia groups for violating their terms of service.

Media coverage of these environments includes descriptions of the virtual crime that takes place online and concerns about the content of such environments. One recent case, involving a virtual paedophile ring in second life, illustrates this concern. Journalists revealed a hidden virtual playground within second life in which avatars designed to look like children offered visitors sex. Despite restrictions on membership stating that second life is intended to have an over 18 population, the wonderland case raised concerns that activities within this online environment might encourage harm against children in the real world.

Online Gaming

The internet presents children and teens with a range of online gaming entertainment. One increasingly popular phenomenon involves online multiplayer games which may be joined by paying monthly subscription fees. Like the online worlds described above, the involve avatars and immersive two or three dimensional worlds, but introduce set activities and teamwork. Participants begin by creating an avatar and then make their way though levels, increasing their avatar's strength and experience by successfully completing tasks and/or defeating enemies in combat. One key aspect of these games is the social nature of the game play offered, with participants joining forces in clans and guilds. Game play is often supplemented by chat, and teamwork and social interactions are a significant aspect of the gaming experience.

These games are often referred to as massively multiplayer online games (MMOGs) or massively multiplayer online role-playing games (MMORPGs) a development of earlier paper and pencil role playing games such as Dungeons and Dragons. The most famous MMOG titles include the Sims online, Ultima Online, Everquest and World of Warcraft. The academic literature on online gaming explores a range of issues that have been raised in work on console and PC gaming. However, the social aspect of interacting in these game environments and the repercussions of potentially endless forms of gaming entertainment, introduce new issues and concerns, which have been voiced by the media in different ways. Thus it has been suggested that the potentially open-ended, social and goal-driven nature of online gaming is more likely to lead to gaming addiction.

Here we discusses about the identity of the potential risks and benefits of new and emerging forms of online communication. While some of the risks are clearly familiar from studies of previous cultural forms, others are distinctly new. Some of the positive aspects of these phenomena are only just beginning to appear. In this ever-changing environment, it is important to aware that the consequences of technological developments are by no means guaranteed. Technologies may embody certain constraints and possibilities, but which of these proves to be significant depends to a great extent on how the technologies are used. Here again it is important to recognize that the potentially negative effects of these media may well be inextricable from the positive ones, and that the most significant or pervasive risks may be the ones that are less than immediately obvious.

• • •